4/13/02

To Loretta,

Thanks for your generous
support and for taking the
class.

Affectionately,
Toba

Creative Cookies

Delicious Decorating for Any Occasion

Toba
Garrett

Sterling Publishing Co., Inc.
New York

Edited by Jeanette Green
Designed by Judy Morgan, Jeannine Ford, and Jeanette Green
Illustrated by Wilma Josephs and Toba Garrett
Cookie patterns recreated on computer by Christine Mathews
Photographs by Steven Mark Needham
Proofread by Jessie Leaman

Library of Congress Cataloging-in-Publication Data

Garrett, Toba.
 Creative cookies : delicious decorating for any occasion / Toba Garrett.
  p. cm.
 Includes index.
 ISBN 0–8069–3698–3
  1. Cookies. 2. Garnishes (Cookery) I. Title.
 TX772.G35 2001
 641.8'654—dc21   00–048269

1 3 5 7 9 10 8 6 4 2

Published by Sterling Publishing Company, Inc.
387 Park Avenue South, New York, N.Y. 10016
© 2001 by Toba Garrett
Distributed in Canada by Sterling Publishing
^c/o Canadian Manda Group, One Atlantic Avenue, Suite 105
Toronto, Ontario, Canada M6K 3E7
Distributed in Great Britain and Europe by Cassell PLC
Wellington House, 125 Strand, London WC2R 0BB, England
Distributed in Australia by Capricorn Link (Australia) Pty Ltd.
P.O. Box 6651, Baulkham Hills, Business Centre, NSW 2153, Australia
Printed in China
All rights reserved

ISBN 0-8069-3698-3

For James and Phoenix,
the two men in my life

Chicquetta, Valerie, and Kartrell,
my siblings

George Edward,
my dad,
and
Sarah Elizabeth,
my beloved mother

Special Thanks

Without the generous support and help of these people, this book could not have been written. I owe them all a great deal of thanks and sincere gratitude: Sheila Anne Barry, Steven Mark Needham, Arlene P. Bluth, Dr. and Mrs. Sheldon Rabin, Wilma Josephs, Chris Mathews, Jeanette Green, my editor, and Jeannine Ford, Sterling's associate art director.

I also want to thank Colette Peters, Stephanie Sutow, Rosemary Littman, Dona Bianco, John Mangeri, Nick Malgieri, and Tonessa West Crowe, who first introduced me to this amazing art

Contents

Introduction

$\mathcal{E}$ver since I can remember, I have been fascinated with the joy of baking. I have delighted in the many varieties of mouthwatering cookies and cakes. While growing up, I helped my grandmother and mother in the kitchen whenever I could—especially when flour, sugar, fresh eggs, and sweet butter were the main ingredients. As the smell of baking goodies filled the house, I eagerly anticipated those first bites.

My family often prepared baked goodies for special occasions, family gatherings, church potluck suppers, and school functions. We always made something delectable for holidays. My favorite holiday was, and still is, Thanksgiving. I love the smell of cloves, ginger, and other spices in wonderful pies and cookies. Although many families no longer bake in the traditional ways once enjoyed by our parents and grandparents, most of us still have favorite baking activities. I bake potato and custard pies, and I always like to have an assortment of cookies on hand.

Cookie-making is great fun for me, and I'm sure, if it isn't already, it will be for you, too. It helps ease stress and allows you to quietly control something that's all your own. You don't even have to be a baking expert; a few simple recipes will allow a wonderful range of creative possibilities. You can bake cookies on your own schedule—even well ahead of time, if you wish. Just refrigerate or freeze them so that they will be ready for all kinds of parties and occasions.

They make great gifts when wrapped in pretty boxes with ribbons. They are always a delightful treat to enjoy when unexpected guests or family members arrive.

Just dust a little powdered sugar, cinnamon, or cocoa powder on cookies brought to room temperature from your refrigerator or freezer. You can also decorate them with chocolate shavings curled with a vegetable peeler; sugared orange and lemon peels; toasted and slivered almonds; glazes of Sieved Apricot Jam; or currants, shredded coconut, or candy. Even a simple icing can make a cookie appear as well-dressed and formal as cake. Whatever kind of tasty decoration you choose, you can create a dramatic effect with a few simple tricks. Then serve your creations on a drop-dead fancy plate or platter that will make your guests beg for more.

Did you ever receive cookies in a box that was more impressive than the cookies themselves? Perhaps the cookies didn't taste as good as you'd hoped or they weren't distinctive enough for that important family or business function. Baking and custom designing your own cookies can mean that the cookies' taste and presentation are even more wonderful than the perfect box you found for them.

Decorating cookies is something everyone— even young children—can do. It is not as intimidating as decorating a cake, and you can eat the mistakes. Just make the cookies a few days ahead, buy the fun stuff for decoration, and whip up an incredibly simple cookie icing. The excitement begins when you put everything together. You can be as creative as you wish, and you can have twice as much fun when family and friends help. If you have natural decorating skills, the possibilities are endless.

Beautifully decorated cookies can be used for any occasion; they don't need to be targeted to a specific holiday. These cookies are a welcome treat on Valentine's Day, Mother's Day, Father's Day, Halloween, Thanksgiving, Christmas, Kwanzaa, birthdays, anniversaries, bar mitzvahs, bat mitzvahs, and any event where desserts would naturally be included. They can also be served in corporate dining rooms, taken to a friend in the hospital, passed around at office parties, offered at intermission of a play or concert, or added to a restaurant meal.

Cookie decorating can also be its own occasion. You can have a delightful party for children when each child dons an apron and decorates his or her own cookies.

Cookies have universal appeal and they can be presented in many different ways. Nearly everyone (except a few curmudgeons lacking a sweet tooth) loves receiving and eating them. When the recipient realizes that you made this gift with loving care, your cookies will be much more special.

It just takes a little extra attention to make your cookies beautiful. With a little practice, they can be stunning, and for those who possess a critical eye, a love for detail, and lots of patience—your cookies can look like works of art!

Basic Techniques

With a little practice, you'll be able to use decorating equipment, prepare dough and icing, and make a pastry cone like an expert. You'll master decorating techniques like flooding and outlining cookies as well as stitching, piping embroidery, gilding, using a stencil, adding borders, piping lace, making plunger flowers, and much more.

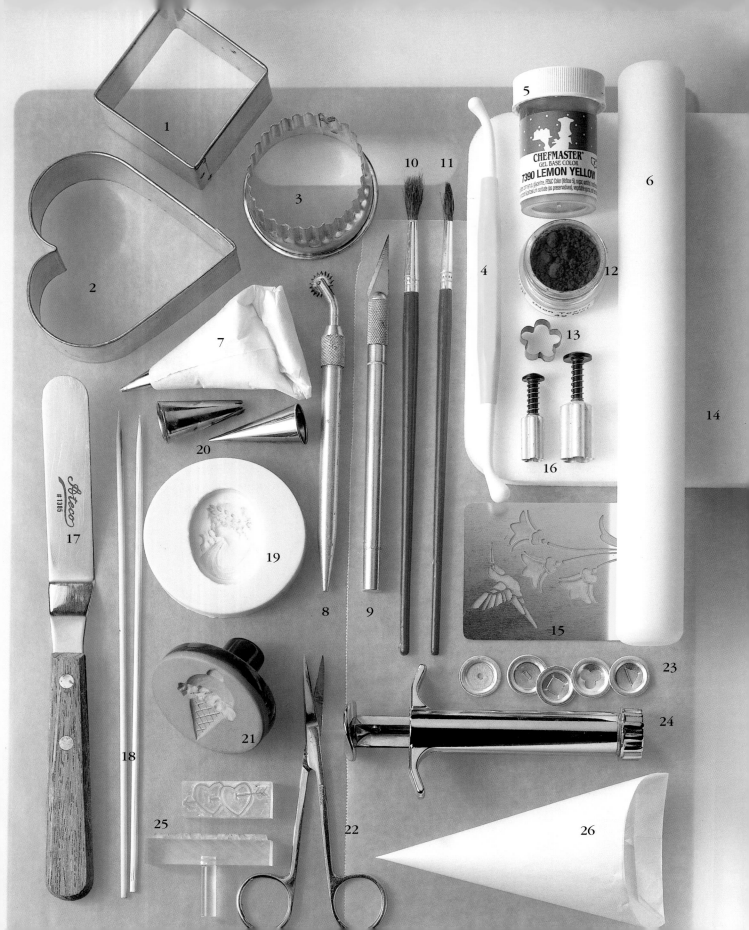

Equipment

I've used a heavy-duty stationary mixer to make all the cookie and icing recipes. However, you can use a handheld mixer if you cut the recipes in half.

You'll need several stainless-steel bowls, rubber spatulas, liquid and dry measuring cups, measuring spoons, a paring knife, a cutting board, a wooden rolling pin, and a large selection of metal or plastic cookie cutters.

Here are some cookie-decorating tools you'll want to own. Many of them are shown in the photo on p. 10. You can find them in specialty cake-decorating, kitchen-supply, and craft stores.

Cookie Cutters   Standard equipment in most kitchens, cookie cutters are used for cutting out cookie dough and rolled icings.

Dog-Bone Tool   This tool is used primarily to soften the edges of petals and leaves made of Rolled Fondant, quick gum paste, and white and dark modeling chocolate.

Paste Food Colors and Gel Food Colors   These professional-strength colors (food coloring), used for coloring icings and fondants, are sold in cake-decorating and craft stores.

Nonstick Rolling Pin   This small white rolling pin for rolled icings can be used for making flowers and leaves.

Wooden Rolling Pin   The traditional wooden rolling pin is great for rolling out cookie dough and rolled icings.

Quilting Wheel   The wheel gives a "stitch" effect on the edge of a rolled-icing cookie and can be used to create quilting techniques.

Precision Knife   Also known as an X-acto knife, this knife is preferred when cutting a trace pattern on cookie dough. It's perfect for an accurate cut of rolled icings. A #11 blade works well; cut using the pointed tip.

Paintbrushes   Paintbrushes are essential for food-color painting or petal dusting on fondant or for icing flowers. Sable brushes are good for most painting. Chinese brushes are the best for brush painting. Your brushes should range from #000, 00, and 0 to #1, 3, and 5. You'll also need a good filbert brush and a few small to medium-large brushes for dry dusting.

Petal Dust   Nontoxic powder colors are used primarily on gum-paste flowers and rolled icings. These come in hundreds of colors and are available at cake-decorating stores.

Five-Petal Cutters & Plunger Cutters   A small five-petal blossom cutter can be used to make baby's breath as well as apple, cherry, and orange blossoms. These cutters and dozens of other cutters in various sizes can be found in cake-decorating and craft stores.

Decorating Equipment (photo opposite)

1 square cutter	7 filled cone and tip	13 five-petal cutter	20 piping tips
2 heart cutter	8 quilting wheel	14 cell pad	21 cookie stamp
3 round cutter	9 precision knife	15 stencil	22 embroidery scissors
4 dog-bone tool	10 flat paintbrush	16 plunger cutters	23 clay-gun disks
5 paste food color(ing)	11 pointed paintbrush	17 offset metal spatula	24 clay gun
6 nonstick rolling pin	12 petal-dust colors	18 wooden skewers	25 impression stamps
		19 silicone mold	26 parchment cone

Cell Pad A small white or black pad (a little softer than a piece of Styrofoam) can be used to help soften the edges of petals and leaves made out of gum paste or rolled icings.

Stencils Stencils help you create a quick and beautiful design with no effort. They're sold in craft and hobby stores.

Piping Tips Metal tips are used for accurate piping of royal icing. (We have two recipes, Meringue Powder Royal Icing and Egg White Royal Icing.) You'll want a range of tips, including #0, 1, 2, 3, 4, 5, 6, 18, and 67.

Offset Metal Spatula Essential in any kitchen, this tool helps you mix icings, move cut-out cookies, and handle rolled icing dough. You should have several small, a few medium, and two extra-large spatulas.

Rounded Toothpicks & Skewers Toothpicks and skewers can be used to color royal and rolled icings. They're also valuable in ruffling rolled icing and in scoring veins in leaves made of gum paste and other rolled icings.

Silicone Molds Molds can create lovely textured designs on cakes and cookies. You'll find them at most cake-decorating and craft stores, but some specialty items are only available at select suppliers.

Cookie Stamps If you use a cookie stamp for pressing a design into cookie dough before it's baked, you don't have to decorate the cookie later.

Embroidery Scissors Little scissors are great for cutting out patterns and helpful for making small gum-paste flowers.

Clay Gun & Disks Use the clay gun to make rope, tassels, and other decorative designs. You'll find the gun and disks in art, hobby, and cake-decorating stores. It's called a clay gun because it's used to shape clay used by potters. The small gun is made of metal and much smaller and more precise than the cookie presses you may be familiar with.

Impression & Embossing Stamps Stamps can create beautiful designs in rolled icings. Select a variety of them from your favorite cake-decorating and craft stores.

Parchment Paper & Cones Parchment cones are essential to any cookie or cake decorator. Parchment paper can be used to roll out cookie and icing dough; it's also great for tracing and baking on designs. Cones are great for piping small and large projects, and they make cleanup easy. You can throw away the bag after using it.

Polyurethane Cones These piping cones can be washed and reused. The disadvantage is that any added food color may not wash out and will stain the cone and may affect the color of the next icing.

Palette Knife A palette knife is excellent for getting under a dry, flooded plaque or for picking up thinly rolled gum paste or fondant icings.

Liquid Whitener This is a chalk-white color in a liquid form. Use a little of this and mix it with paste and gel food colors to obtain beautiful pastel shades. It's great for painting.

Mixer A heavy-duty mixer is essential if you plan to make cookies and ice them often. A handheld mixer can be used if you make half-recipes of cookie dough and icings.

Dough Preparation

Dough

Have all the ingredients ready, i.e., butter, sugar, eggs, flour, baking powder, salt, extracts, spices, etc. Consult the Measurements section (pages 140–141) for how to measure ingredients with precision. A kitchen scale can be helpful.

Carefully follow directions for making the cookie dough. Note any special hints for the specific recipe, e.g., if the dough can be rolled out right away or if it needs to be refrigerated. Check recipes to see if you can make the dough ahead of time.

The butter should be slightly moist on the outside but cold on the inside. Take the butter out of the refrigerator 20 to 30 minutes before you make the dough. In warm weather, take the butter out about 15 minutes before preparing the dough.

Once you have prepared the dough, divide it in half and shape each half into a round disk about 4 to 5 inches (10 to 12.5 cm) in diameter. Wrap each half in plastic wrap until you're ready to use it.

Roll & Cut

Have all your tools ready. Get out the rolling pin, extra flour for rolling, the long metal offset spatula, cookie cutters, and everything else you'll need.

When you're ready to roll, lightly dust the surface you'll be using with the same kind of flour you've used to make the dough. If the dough is firm, you don't need much flour. However, if the dough is soft, you may need a little more flour. Be careful not to add too much flour because it may alter the dough and make the cookie tough.

If you just took the dough out of the refrigerator, let it sit for 15 minutes and apply firm pressure when rolling. If the dough was made just moments ago, apply light to medium pressure when rolling. Roll out the dough to the required thickness (generally ⅛ inch or 0.3 cm thick unless otherwise noted). Roll the dough, turning it each time you roll up and down (Step 1).

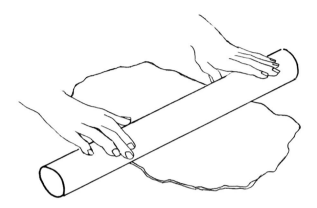

STEP 1. Roll out the dough.

The larger you roll out the dough, the more difficult it will be to turn the dough each time. At this point, you can run a large metal offset spatula under the dough to prevent it from sticking (Step 2). Before you slide it under the dough, dip the spatula into the flour.

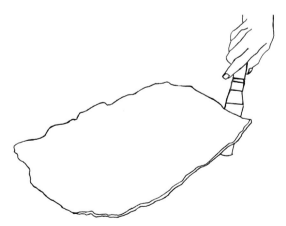

STEP 2. Slide an offset metal spatula under the dough to prevent sticking.

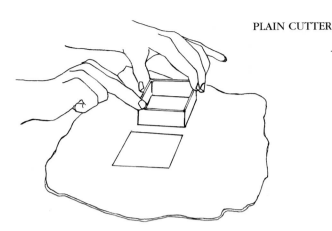 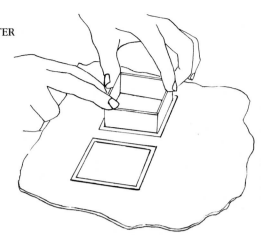

STEP 3. Cut the dough with a cookie cutter.   STEP 4. Score the border using a smaller cutter.

When the dough is the required thickness, dip the cookie cutter into the flour and cut the dough. Move the cutter in the dough slightly to make sure that you have separated the cookie shape from the rest of the dough (Step 3). Make all the required cuts. Remove the excess dough.

When you're ready to transfer the cookies to a pan, use a large, flat spatula and carefully place them on an ungreased nonstick cookie sheet or a parchment-lined half-sheet pan. Make sure that you have at least a ½-inch (1.25-cm) space around each cookie.

Scoring Cookies

When scoring cookies, look for cookie cutters in varying sizes of the same family. Use a slightly smaller cutter and place it over the larger cut-out cookie. Lightly impress the cutter into the cut dough to make a border slightly smaller than the cookie around the perimeter.

This scored border will be helpful when you outline the cookie, giving you a guide as you pipe (Step 4). If your cookie shape requires a scalloped cutter, use a plain round cutter for the inside edge to make it easier to create an outline.

SCALLOPED CUTTER

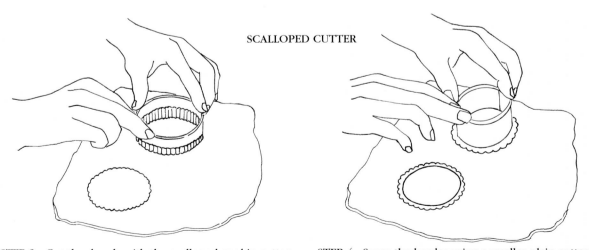

STEP 3. Cut the dough with the scalloped cookie cutter.   STEP 4. Score the border using a smaller plain cutter.

Parchment Cone

Making the Parchment Cone

Cut paper into an equilateral triangle (all three sides measure the same) or buy triangular-cut paper. Mark asterisks at the triangle's top corner and at its left and right corners. Put two pieces of masking tape on the back of your right (or writing) hand. Hold the triangle like a pyramid with the peak (corner A) pointing away from you, or "north" if we were to use a map's N–S–E–W orientation (Step 1).

With your left hand, bring the bottom left corner B up to meet the top corner A or "north"

peak (Step 2). Place corner B directly on top of the north peak A with the ends directly over each other (no overlapping).

Put a piece of tape over the seam so that it won't come apart. You'll probably need to turn it around toward you to tape it (Step 3).

Then bring corner C completely around the cone and up to where corners A and B meet (Step 4). Make sure that all the seams are dead center. All three asterisks should be lined up together. Put a piece of tape over the right corner seam, sealing all the seams. Fold about 2 inches (5 cm) of flap on the inside to finish the cone.

The finished cone is shown on p. 16 (top left); you'll also see it with or without a metal tip.

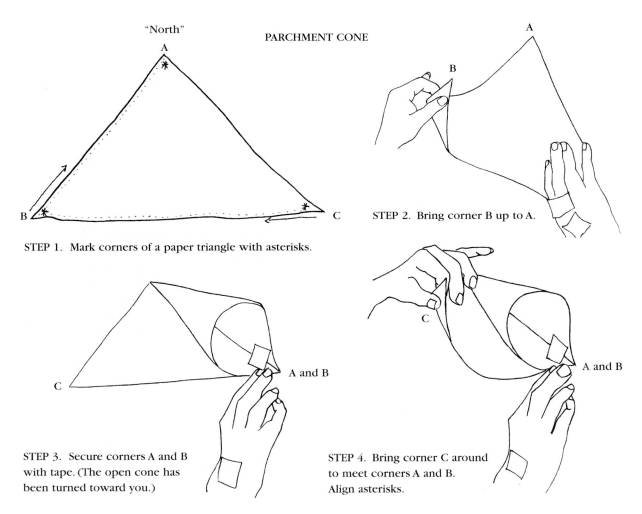

PARCHMENT CONE

"North"

STEP 1. Mark corners of a paper triangle with asterisks.

STEP 2. Bring corner B up to A.

STEP 3. Secure corners A and B with tape. (The open cone has been turned toward you.)

STEP 4. Bring corner C around to meet corners A and B. Align asterisks.

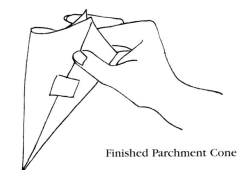

Finished Parchment Cone

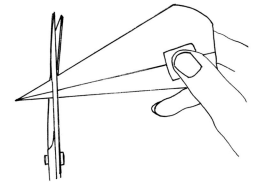

Cut Cone for a Metal Tip

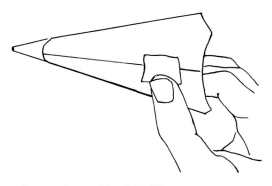

Parchment Cone with a Metal Tip

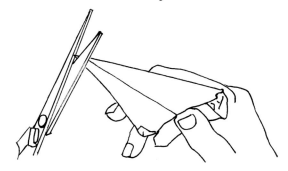

Small Cut for Cone without a Metal Tip

Filling a Parchment Cone with Icing

WITH A METAL TIP

Cut a ½-inch (1.25-cm) piece of the cone (from the point end) with a pair of scissors (see Cut Cone for a Metal Tip, left). Drop a tip (usually a #2, 3, or 4 when outlining) into the parchment cone. The metal tip should extend at least a ½ inch (1.25 cm) from the bottom of the cone (see Parchment Cone with a Metal Tip). Add 1 tablespoon of icing inside the cone and pull down on the bag so that the icing fills up all air spaces. Fold the cone from the left side over the center, and then from the right side over the center. Fold the top toward the seam twice.

WITHOUT A METAL TIP

Don't cut the parchment cone if you are going to do outline or flood work without a tip. Simply put a tablespoon of icing inside the bag. Pull down on the bag so that the icing fills up all air spaces. Fold the cone from the left side over the center, and then from the right side over the center. Fold the top two times to seal the icing inside. Finally, when you're ready to pipe or flood, cut a small opening in the cone (Small Cut for Cone without a Metal Tip).

The cone with a metal tip is filled with Meringue Powder Royal Icing and ready to use. Glacé Icing is in the bowl.

Decorating Techniques

While you're piping or using another decorating technique, use plastic wrap to cover the bowl of icing. Also wrap rolled icing. That way, your icing won't dry out as quickly.

How to Color Icing

Icings: Rolled Fondant, White Modeling Chocolate, and Quick Gum Paste pages 131, 133, and 139
Coloring: Paste Food Color or Gel Food Color

Rolled Icing When coloring Rolled Fondant, White Modeling Chocolate, and Quick Gum Paste, add a little paste or gel food color (food coloring) on a toothpick. Wipe it on the paste. Knead the paste until the desired color is achieved. If the paste gets sticky or moist, knead in a little cornstarch to absorb extra moisture. If the paste is dry, add a little white vegetable shortening.

Meringue Powder Royal Icing & Glacé Icing Add even less color on a toothpick when coloring a soft or creamy icing.

Rolled Icing

To cover a cookie with rolled icing, roll the icing to ⅛ inch (0.3 cm) thick. Dust the cookie surface lightly with cornstarch or powdered sugar if you plan to use Rolled Fondant or White Modeling Chocolate. Dust it with cocoa powder if you plan to use Dark Modeling Chocolate. You'll find recipes for three rolled icings, Rolled Fondant, Chocolate Rolled Fondant, and White, Milk, and Dark Modeling Chocolate, on pages 131–133.

Cut with the same cutter used to cut the cookies. Note that the icing will be slightly larger than the cookie because the cookie will shrink slightly during baking (see Cutting Out Rolled Icing on page 18).

Before placing the rolled icing onto the cookie, brush the cookie with light corn syrup or Sieved Apricot Jam (page 139). Carefully place the rolled icing onto the cookie.

Note: Several icings come under the heading of rolled icing, such as White Rolled Fondant; Chocolate Rolled Fondant; White, Milk, or Dark Modeling Chocolate. The Rolled Fondant used in this book is called Pettinice RTR Icing; it's a ready-to-use commercial icing that can be rolled thin, ruffled, and shaped into small flowers.

Glacé Icing tinted with gel food color (small bowls left) and Meringue Powder Royal Icing (largest bowl right).

White Rolled Fondant and Dark Modeling Chocolate are rolled icings that can be cut into a desired shape.

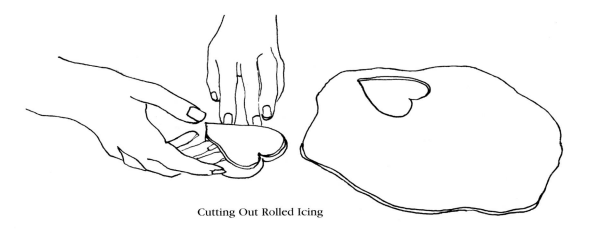

Cutting Out Rolled Icing

The sides of this cookie "box" are covered with rolled icing. The ribbon is also made of rolled icing. The lid was covered with rolled icing, outlined, and brush painted.

Outlining

Position the bag at the point where you want to begin outlining. A right-handed person pipes counterclockwise—starting at the 9 o'clock position of the circle. A left-handed person pipes clockwise—starting at 3 o'clock.

Apply even pressure at a 45° angle. Touch the cookie surface and squeeze. Gently lift up the bag about 1 to 1½ inches (2.5 to 3.75 cm) from the surface. Let icing fall as you move your hands (using the cookie's perimeter as a guide). As you go around the perimeter of the cookie, begin to lower your hands so that the end of the icing meets the beginning of the outline (Piping the Outline).

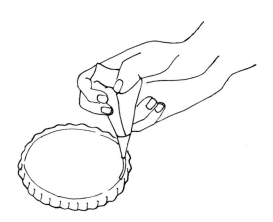

Piping the Outline

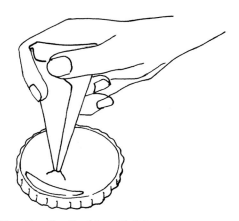

Flooding the Cookie with Icing

Flooding the Cookie

Cut a small hole in the cone that contains the flood icing. Start in the center and squeeze the bag, keeping the tip of the cone inside the outline of icing as you squeeze and move the bag near the cookie's perimeter. Don't squeeze out too much icing (see Flooding the Cookie with Icing on page 18).

Stick the toothpick into the flood icing to move the icing toward the outline, working quickly so that the icing doesn't start to set up before you have covered every crevice of the surface (Using a Toothpick for Flooding). Remove the toothpick. Don't touch the cookie. Allow the icing to set for at least 20 to 25 minutes before you carefully slide a metal offset spatula under the cookie to move it. Allow the cookie to dry completely. This can take from 2 to 4 hours (surface dry) or 6 to 12 hours (hard dry).

Outline & Flood on Paper

Designs can be outlined and flooded directly on paper and later transferred onto an iced cookie. First, trace the design on parchment or tracing paper. Place the traced pattern on a piece of Plexiglas or a hard surface. Cover the pattern with a piece of plastic wrap. Tape the corners securely with masking tape. Outline and flood the design.

Wait for 2 to 4 hours (for a surface dry) or 6 to 12 hours (for a hard dry). For a very large design—over 4 to 8 inches (10 to 20 cm) in diameter—you may need to dry the design for 12 to 24 hours, depending on the type of flood icing used.

When it has dried, carefully remove the design from the paper by sliding a pallet knife under the design. Secure the design onto the cookie with a few drops of outline icing. Or carefully remove the taped ends and gently pull the paper over the Plexiglas edge or surface edge. As you pull the paper, the design will move forward. Carefully remove the design with a large metal offset spatula and attach to the cookie with a few drops of outline icing.

Flooding Figures & Flowers

When flooding a design with several components, such as a flower, a bird, cartoon characters, or more, it is important to flood each component of the design separately. That way, you'll allow each part of the design to crust over. This is important if you are flooding a five-petal flower and you want each petal to stand out instead of their blending together. Flood every other petal first. Then let each petal dry for 15 minutes. Then flood the neighboring petals.

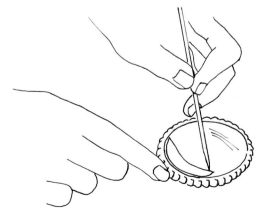

Using a Toothpick for Flooding

This apple-shaped cookie was outlined with white Glacé Outline Icing and flooded with red Glacé Icing.

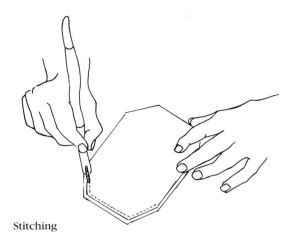
Stitching

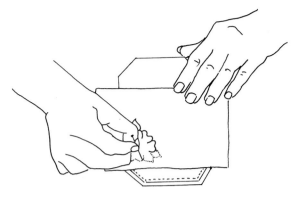
Pinprick Method

Stitching

Icing: Rolled Icing ▦ pages 131–133

Stitching is a beautiful design on a cookie using Rolled Icing. Usually, stitching is done around the perimeter of the icing, but it can also be used to create beautiful cross-stitching or quilting effects on a cookie covered with rolled icing.

Once the cookie is covered with the Rolled Icing, position the quilting tool on the edge of the cookie about ¹⁄₁₆ to ⅛ inch (0.15 to 0.3 cm) from the outside edge of the icing and apply gentle but firm pressure to create stitching that outlines the cookie (see Stitching).

"Stitching" appears around the shirts of the gingerbread boy and girl.

Transferring a Design

Find a manageable design to display on your cookie. With rolled icing, the design can be transferred immediately. However, a flooded cookie should be completely dry before transferring a design.

Pinprick Method for Rolled Icing

Icing: Rolled Icing ▦ pages 131–133

To transfer the design, take a piece of see-through paper (such as parchment or tracing paper) and trace the design to be transferred. Place the pattern on the cookie. With a straight pin, prick the outline onto the cookie (see Pinprick Method). Outline and flood the design.

Carbon-Copy Method for Flood Icing

Icing: Meringue Powder Flood Icing ▦ page 136

To transfer the design, take a piece of see-through paper (such as parchment or tracing paper) and trace the design to be transferred. Turn the paper over and trace the opposite side of the paper. Turn the paper right side up and place it on the iced cookie. With a #2 graphite pencil, retrace the cookie. Lift up the paper to reveal a carbon copy of the design. Outline and flood the cookie. This technique can also be used on a rolled-icing cookie.

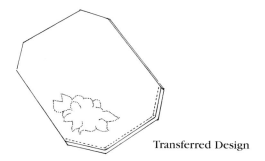

Transferred Design

Note: Pencils made from graphite are nontoxic and considered safe to consume. In such minute quantities, the graphite will not affect the cookie's taste.

Embroidery Piping

Icing: Egg White Royal Icing or Meringue Powder Royal Icing ▢ pages 134 and 135

To achieve a natural look, fine embroidery is always piped freehand. Use the technique of dragging the tip on the surface lightly as you pipe the designs. The tip should be held at a 45° angle. You should have an even flow of pressure as you pipe. Before piping the embroidery designs on the cookies, practice on paper or, if you hate to waste the icing, something edible.

Embroidery piping can create monograms, flowers, and other designs that resemble hand sewing on cloth. The outer edges with "C" scrolls were piped freehand.

Gilding

Special Purchase: Powdered "Gold" and Lemon Extract

Gilding is a technique for mixing powdered gold and a small amount of alcohol or lemon extract to achieve a liquid product. With a small sable brush, you can brush this "liquid gold" onto any surface that you want illuminated.

The gold powder used in this book and sold in decorating stores is not real gold. It's a nontoxic powder. In small quantities, the powder will have no effect on the taste or digestion. Mix ½ teaspoon of powdered gold with a few drops of lemon extract. Stir with a small brush until you have a liquid solution. Use a sable paintbrush to brush on icing or cameos. When the alcohol evaporates, the gold turns into a solid. Add a few more drops of extract to convert it back into a liquid state.

Unlike gold powder, *gold leaf* is actually 95.6% gold. This expensive decoration is quite edible.

The gilding on these chocolate rose petals adds highlights and creates a more natural appearance.

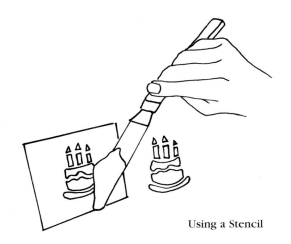

Using a Stencil

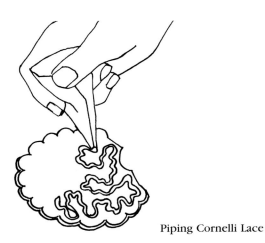

Piping Cornelli Lace

Using a Stencil

Icings: Meringue Powder Royal Icing and Glacé Icing ▬ pages 135 and 137

When using a stencil on a cookie iced with Glacé Icing, make sure that the icing is hard dry. Place the stencil over the cookie. Use a palette knife or small offset metal spatula to remove a small amount of medium-consistency Meringue Powder Royal Icing. Position the knife at a 45° angle and drag the knife over the stencil. If you miss any of the design in the stencil, go over the stencil again (see Using a Stencil). Carefully remove the stencil from the cookie. Immediately clean the stencil with a damp cloth.

Cornelli Lace

Icing: Meringue Powder Royal Icing ▬ page 135

Cornelli lace is a simple technique used to enhance any decorated cookie. This technique can be applied before the icing sets or after the icing has completely dried. Half-fill a small parchment cone with Meringue Powder Royal Icing; use a #1 metal piping tip. Hold the bag perpendicular to the iced cookie. Touch the surface of the icing and gently squeeze. Lift the bag about 1 inch (2.5 cm) from the surface and let the icing fall. Move your hands in a swirling motion, remembering not to let the icing cross over.

Stencil (left) and stencil work on cookies (right).

White Cornelli lace gives this cookie texture.

Cornelli lace should be one continuous line; however, that can be difficult to achieve. If you need to break the line and start at another point in the design, end the line near the cookie's outline or perimeter. Start a new line and continue (see Piping Cornelli Lace on page 22).

For a loose look, use a larger—#2 or #3—round tip. Pipe the design, making a wider swirl.

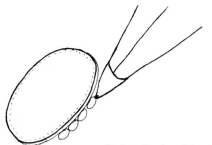

Piping Oval and Snail Borders

Swiss Dots

Icing: Meringue Powder Royal Icing ▬ page 135

Swiss dots are a simple but effective design that can add dimension to a flat surface.

Take 2 tablespoons of Royal Icing and add ½ teaspoon to 1 full teaspoon of water to soften the icing. The idea is to create an icing that's between firm and flood consistency. Put the icing in a small parchment cone. When ready to pipe, snip a tiny hole in the cone. (Flooding does not require use of a metal tip inside the cone.)

Position the tip of the cone at the surface of the cookie and apply the lightest pressure—forming a round dot. Pull away. As you pull away, the tip of the icing will shrink back into a round ball (instead of forming a peak at the tip).

Ovals & Snails

Icing: Meringue Powder Royal Icing ▬ page 135

Load a parchment bag with a #3, 4, or 5 round metal tip. Add 1 tablespoon of Meringue Powder Royal Icing. Hold the tip at a 45° angle. Apply pressure, allowing some icing to protrude through the tip. Move the tip forward slightly; then pull the tip toward you, easing off the pressure. Scratch the tip on the surface as you pull toward you and stop. Position the tip about ¼ inch (0.6 cm) in back of the previous oval and start the next oval, pushing forward slightly and touching the tip of the previous oval. Pull forward and ease off the pressure. Continue until you have piped a bead around a cameo or a border around a cookie (see Piping Oval and Snail Borders).

Swiss dots appear on this little house.

White ovals form an elegant border around the cameo.

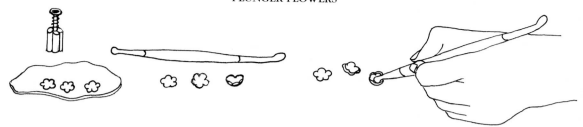

Five-petal blossom cutter or plunger (upper left) and rolled icing with cut-out flowers (lower left).
A dog-bone tool (left center and in hand right) can cup the plunger flowers (right).

Plunger Flowers

Icing: Rolled Fondant and Meringue Powder Royal Icing ▬ pages 131 and 135

These flowers can be made out of Rolled Fondant (prepared with Pettinice RTR Icing). Make them up in abundance and keep them on hand for quick decorating.

Dust the cookie surface with a little cornstarch. Roll out the icing to ⅛ inch (0.3 cm) thick. Use a miniature five-petal blossom cutter and cut out many flowers (above left). Place flowers on a cell pad and gently cups the flower with a dog-bone or ball tool (above right). Pipe a dot in the center with Meringue Powder Royal Icing. When they are dry, dust the flowers with petal dust.

These lavender plunger flowers are fairly easy to make with a five-petal cutter, a dog-bone tool, and icing.

The rosettes (left) were hand piped, and the gum-paste flowers (right) were carefully shaped by hand. Both are more difficult and time-consuming to create than plunger flowers.

Cookie Designs

You'll discover textured designs and cookie works of art as well as cookie designs suitable for special occasions, themes, holidays, and love and romance. Family and friends cannot help but admire and savor your cookie tidings.

House & Garden Parties

Webbing is a lovely design that's easy to master. These cookies are appropriate for gift-giving, social gatherings, house or garden parties, and afternoon teas.

Icing: Glacé Icing and Glacé Outline Icing pages 137 and 138
Suggested Cookie: Butter Cookies or Almond Paste Cookies pages 124 and 126

PROCEDURE

Follow the recipe directions for making Butter Cookies or Almond Paste Cookies. Trace a pattern and place it on the rolled-out dough. Cut carefully with an X-acto knife or use cookie cutters in similar shapes. Bake and cool the cookies according to directions. When ready to ice, make two icings, Glacé Icing and Glacé Outline Icing.

Single Web

Select any shape of cookie cutters approximately 2½ to 3 inches (6.25 to 7.5 cm) in diameter. Next, outline the cookies with Glacé Outline Icing. Fill several parchment cones with different colored Glacé Icings.

At the left side of the cookie, pipe vertical lines of icing close to the outline—from top to bottom—about ⅛ to ¼ inch (0.16 to 0.3 cm) wide. Take another bag of icing and pipe a line parallel to it. Pipe a third line, following the procedures for the first and second lines.

Repeat the pattern of three lines of icing, using the same colors, until you are at the right edge of the outlined cookie. Or pipe horizontal lines of icing, using the same technique described for vertical lines (see Single Web).

Single Web. Pipe horizontal or vertical lines of icing.

Use a toothpick to extend the icing and fill up the spaces between each line and from the top to the bottom of the cookie.

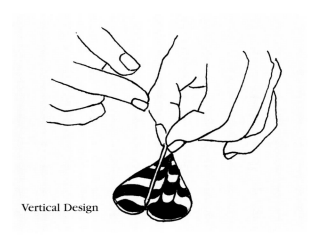

Vertical Design

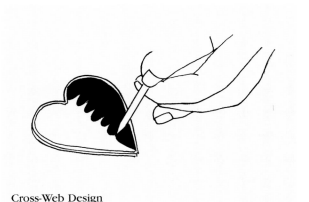

Cross-Web Design

Now position the toothpick at the cookie's top left corner. Stick the toothpick into the icing and drag it to the right, forming a web pattern. Once you reach the right edge, bring the toothpick slightly down and drag it to the left. Repeat the pattern until you run out of space.

To add to the beauty of a single-web design, pipe random dots in Glacé Icing.

For a vertical design, draw a toothpick from the top to the bottom. Once you reach the bottom, lift up the toothpick, start again at the top, and repeat the same process (see Vertical Design).

Double Web

For a double-web design, turn a single-web cookie clockwise one-quarter turn. Position the toothpick at the top left corner and create a single-web pattern.

Cross Web

Use a cookie with a marked outline. Fill in half of the cookie with a dark color of Glacé Icing and fill in the other half with a lighter color of Glacé Icing. Begin at the cookie's left side using the darkest color of icing and drag a toothpick to pull the darker shade of icing into the light shade. (Do NOT REVERSE THE PATTERN.) Lift the toothpick out of the light shade of icing, and repeat the pattern of moving the dark color into the light color (see Cross-Web Design).

Double Web with Vertical Design

Cross Web

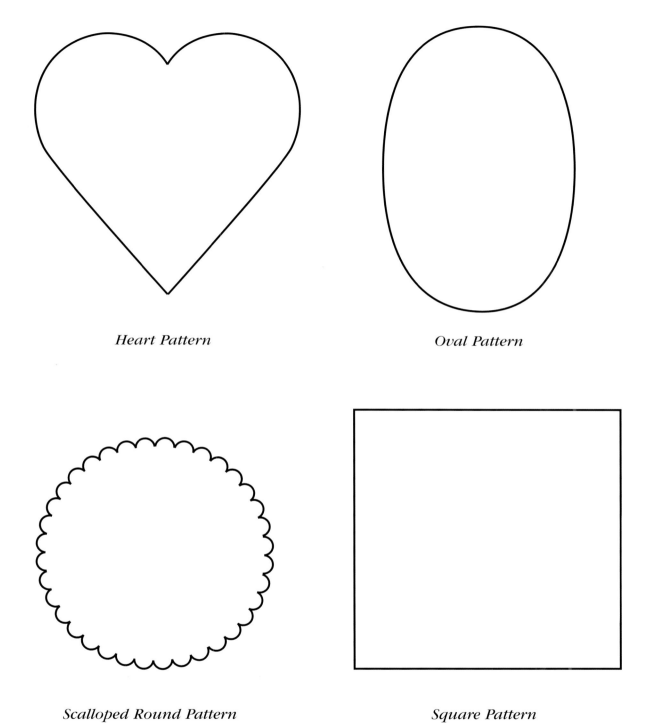

Heart Pattern

Oval Pattern

Scalloped Round Pattern

Square Pattern

Birthdays

These designs are easy and delightful. Make this a group effort using a variety of stencils.

Icing: Glacé Icing and Meringue Powder Royal Icing ▦ pages 137 and 135
Suggested Cookie: Butter Cookies ▦ page 124

PROCEDURE

Follow the recipe directions for making Butter Cookies. Trace the cookie pattern, and place it on the rolled-out dough. Cut carefully with an X-acto knife or use cookie cutters in similar shapes. Bake and cool the cookies according to directions. When ready to ice, make two icings, Glacé Icing and Meringue Powder Royal Icing.

Buy stencils with birthday designs. Outline the cookies with Meringue Powder Royal Icing and flood the cookies with Glacé Icing. Pipe two tones in some designs; divide a rectangular cookie in half and flood it with two different colors. Let the cookies dry completely. When they are dry, place the stencil overlay on the cookie (see Birthday Stencil).

With a palette knife or an offset metal spatula, spread the Meringue Powder Royal Icing over the stencil, holding the spatula or palette knife at a 45° angle. Carefully remove the stencil.

Birthday Stencil

Buy a stencil like this one or make your own.

When the icing stencils completely dry, create a variety of designs on the cookies. Pipe "C" scrolls on some cookies, "Birthday Wishes" on others, Cornelli lace on some, numbers on others, and line piping on still others.

Cookie Pattern

"C" Scrolls

Line Piping

Cornelli Lace

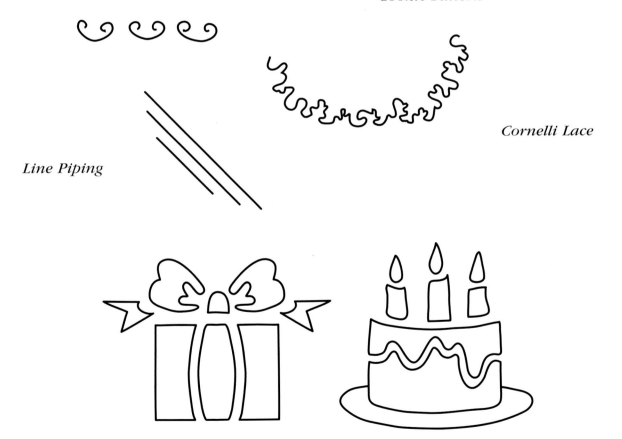

Birthday Stencils

Baby Showers & Christenings

Present these adorable cookies at a baby shower or christening. You can personalize them with a monogram of the baby's or parents' name. Just outline and flood the cookie for a less formal appearance.

Icing: Glacé Icing, Meringue Powder Royal Icing, and Rolled Fondant ▆ pages 137, 135, and 131

Suggested Cookie: Butter Cookies or Shortbread I ▆ pages 124 and 128

PROCEDURE

Follow the recipe directions for making Butter Cookies or Shortbread I. Trace the pattern and place it on the rolled-out dough. Cut carefully with an X-acto knife, or buy cookie cutters in similar shapes. Bake and cool the cookies according to directions. When ready to ice, make three icings, Glacé Icing, Meringue Powder Royal Icing, and Rolled Fondant.

Outline the cookies with Meringue Powder Royal Icing and flood the cookies with Glacé Icing. When the outline and flood icings have dried, practice and then pipe fine embroidery on all the cookies.

Baby Shoe

On the shoe (baby bootie) cookie shape, make tiny ribbon bows and two streamers. Taper the ends of the bows by cutting the ends into a "V" shape (see Ribbon Ends). Secure with Meringue

Powder Royal Icing and place small silver dragées (sugar-coated nuts or small silver-colored balls for decorating cakes) in the center.

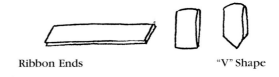

Ribbon Ends   "V" Shape

Baby Bottle

For the bottle cookie, cut two long ribbon streamers and a bow. Soften the edge of the streamers with a dog-bone tool. Make a small ball out of Rolled Fondant and attach it in the center of the bow with Meringue Powder Royal Icing.

With fine embroidery, like the "S" scrolls or decorative dots in groups of three (see page 35), your cookies will be picture perfect.

Baby Bib

For the bib cookie, cut two small streamers. Soften the edge with a dog-bone tool. Attach the ribbon streamers to the top of the bib cookie and twist the streamers (see Streamers). Roll out a piece of Rolled Fondant in a rounded shape in a soft pink, yellow, or blue. Cut the circle in half. Ruffle one of the half circles with a skewer, rounded toothpick, or modeling stick (see Making Ruffles). Attach the ruffles to the bib with a little water. Make a tiny bow and attach it with water or Meringue Powder Royal Icing. Pipe a dot in the center of the bow with Meringue Powder Royal Icing.

Streamers

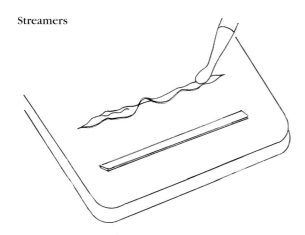

Making Ruffles

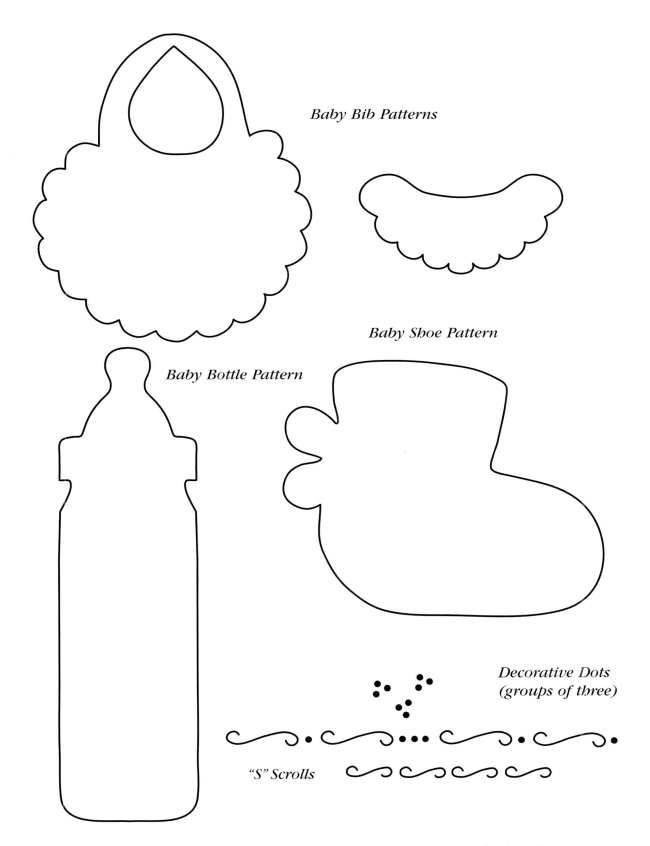

Baby Bib Patterns

Baby Shoe Pattern

Baby Bottle Pattern

Decorative Dots
(groups of three)

"S" Scrolls

Mother's Day

A mother's love is precious. Present her with these unforgettable cameo cookies; she will always remember the special effort you took to make them just right, just for her. And don't forget Grandmother!

Icing: Glacé Icing, Meringue Powder Royal Icing, Rolled Fondant, and White Modeling Chocolate ▪ pages 137, 135, 131, and 133
Additions: Gilding ▪ page 138
Suggested Cookie: Almond Paste Cookies or Shortbread I ▪ pages 126 and 128

PROCEDURE

Follow cookie recipe directions for making Almond Paste Cookies or Shortbread I. Trace the pattern and place it on the rolled-out dough. Cut carefully with an X-acto knife or use cookie cutters in similar shapes. Bake and cool the cookies according to directions. When ready to ice, make four icings, Glacé Icing, Meringue Powder Royal Icing, Rolled Fondant, and White Modeling Chocolate.

Cookies

Ice some cookies with Glacé Icing in a soft peach or pink and some with a deep brown or black. Outline the peach-colored cookies in Glacé Outline Icing; then flood the cookies. Outline the dark brown cookies in Meringue Powder Royal Icing; then flood the cookies.

Cameos

Buy cameo molds from your favorite cake-decorating supplier or craft store. Rub a little white vegetable shortening inside the molds. Knead the Rolled Fondant or White Modeling Chocolate until pliable and elastic. Take a small piece and form it into a round disk shape. Push the small round disk inside the mold (see Cameo Mold, page 38). Turn the mold over and press it on  a hard surface. Carefully remove the paste by pressing both sides of the back of the mold. Let dry for 1 hour. Carefully trim.

Gilding

If you wish, you can gild the cameo with gold (see page 21). Place the cameo on an iced cookie and attach it with a little Meringue Powder Royal Icing. In a small parchment cone, add a #2 round piping tip and 1 tablespoon of Meringue Powder Royal Icing. Pipe beading, making a trail border of ovals and snails (see pages 23 and 38) around the cameo to finish the design.

Embroidery Piping

Mother's Day Heart Pattern

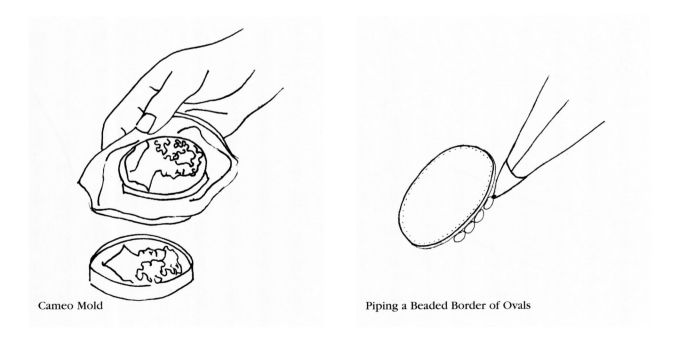

Cameo Mold

Piping a Beaded Border of Ovals

"Get Well" Greetings

Comfort a friend, neighbor, or relative who's under the weather.
Make your own "get-well" cookies, instead of sending a card.
Present these elegantly iced cookies.

Icing: Glacé Icing and Meringue Powder Royal Icing ▬ pages 137 and 135
Suggested Cookie: Butter Cookies or Shortbread I ▬ pages 124 and 128

PROCEDURE

Follow the recipe directions for making Butter Cookies or Shortbread I. Trace the cookie pattern and place it on the rolled-out dough. Cut it out carefully with an X-acto knife, or buy cookie cutters in similar shapes. Bake and cool the cookies according to directions. When you're ready to ice them, make two icings, Glacé Icing and Meringue Powder Royal Icing.

Top Cookie

Outline and flood the cookie. Before the icing sets, pipe a loose Cornelli lace in Glacé Icing over the entire cookie. Let the icing dry 6 to 12 hours. Transfer the "Get Well" greeting onto the cookie by piping the message in Meringue Powder Royal Icing. Gild the message.

Add plunger flowers or a small arrangement of hand-molded filler flowers in a small cluster.

Middle Cookie

Outline and flood the cookie with two-tone colors—one dark and one light. Swirl a toothpick into the icing to create an effect. Before the icing sets, pipe dots in Glacé Icing. Let the icing dry 6 to 12 hours. Transfer the greeting onto the cookie by piping the message in Meringue Powder Royal Icing. Gild the message.

Bottom Cookie

Outline and flood the cookie. Before the icing sets, pipe dots in Glacé Icing. Let the icing dry. Transfer the greeting onto the cookie by piping the message in Meringue Powder Royal Icing. Gild the message. Add plunger flowers or hand-molded filler flowers in small clusters.

Hand-Molded Filler Flowers

got the
bug...

Calligraphy

Get Well
Soon

Feel
Better

Fall Harvest

Fall harvests bring delightful aromas and encourage cozy feelings. Celebrate the fall bounty with these cookies and a hot drink, such as mulled cider, or enjoy them with your Thanksgiving feast.

Icing: Glacé Icing and Meringue Powder Royal Icing   pages 137 and 135
Suggested Cookie: Gingerbread Cookies, Almond Paste Cookies, or Chocolate Cookies   pages 130, 126, and 127

PROCEDURE

Follow the recipe directions for making Gingerbread Cookies, Almond Paste Cookies, or Chocolate Cookies. Trace the cookie patterns and place them on the rolled-out dough. Cut carefully with an X-acto knife or use cookie cutters in similar shapes. Bake and cool the cookies according to directions. When you're ready to ice, make two icings, Glacé Icing and Meringue Powder Royal Icing.

Outline the cookies with brown Meringue Powder Royal Icing. Mix several batches of Glacé Icing in harvest colors, such as pumpkin, gooseberry green, browns, oranges, and more.

Pumpkin

Flood the stem of the pumpkin with brown and green. Flood the rest of the cookie with pumpkin color. Before the icing sets, pipe lines of brown, yellow gold, and a touch of red color into the icing.

Maple Leaves

Flood in green and pumpkin color. Flood the bottoms of the leaves with browns and yellow gold. Before the icing sets, take a toothpick and swirl it around the bottom of the cookie for a more natural look.

Shamrock

Flood with green or gold and flood the bottom with brown. Swirl lightly with a toothpick.

Acorn

Flood the stem with a green color and the rest of the acorn with brown icing. Lightly swirl the green into the brown.

Colors Cues

For pumpkin, mix brown and orange food coloring. For gooseberry, mix leaf-green, brown, and yellow food coloring.

Maple Leaf Pattern

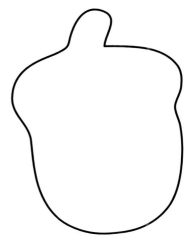

Acorn Pattern

Shamrock Pattern

Pumpkin Pattern

Celebrating Spring

Soothing and refreshing are the colors of spring. This is a nice treat for family or in-laws, after you have completed spring cleaning.

Icing: Rolled Fondant and Meringue Powder Royal Icing ▬ pages 131 and 135
Additions: Paste or Gel Food Colors and Seived Apricot Jam
Suggested Cookie: Lemon & Orange Cream Cookies ▬ page 125

PROCEDURE

Follow the recipe directions for making Lemon & Orange Cream Cookies. Trace the pattern and place it on the rolled-out dough. Use the pinprick or pencil transfer technique.

Cut out cookie shapes carefully with an X-acto knife or use cookie cutters. Bake and cool the cookies according to directions. When ready to ice, make two icings, Rolled Fondant and Meringue Powder Royal Icing.

Cookies

Brush the cookies with Sieved Apricot Jam. Color some Rolled Fondant in a soft pastel color, such as pink, yellow, blue, or lavender. Roll out the dough and cut it with a cookie cutter or cut it out with one of the spring patterns. Carefully place the Rolled Fondant on the glazed cookies.

Use a flat, hard surface (cardboard, marble, etc.) covered with plastic wrap, to outline and flood the birds. After the birds dry (24 hours), carefully lift them with a palette knife and place them on a cookie covered with rolled icing. Use dots of Meringue Powder Royal Icing as "glue" between the rolled icing and the birds. Or the bird design can be transferred directly on the iced cookie by using the tracing technique or the pinprick technique. Then you can outline and flood the birds.

When flooding the design, flood sections at a time. Do not flood two directly connected sections. After the birds dry, paint four-petal flowers with a fine paintbrush.

These four-petal flowers were painted with a brush.

Brush Painting

Practice brush painting on parchment, using leaf shades like moss green, violet, and pink in paste or gel food coloring. Mix a little liquid whitener into the colors to bring out their pastel tones. Use water to create shadows and light in the design (see Brush Painting, right, and follow directions for brush painting on page 113).

When ready to paint, use simple but fluid strokes. Use various shades to paint dots in flower centers and add flower stems.

On the heart-shaped cookie, pipe the word "Spring," using your best penmanship. Paint a few brush strokes to the left of the cookie. Adorn with flowers in pastel tones of pinks and violets in small strokes and add one or more dots in flower centers. Outline the eight-sided figure with Meringue Powder Royal Icing using a #3 round metal piping tip.

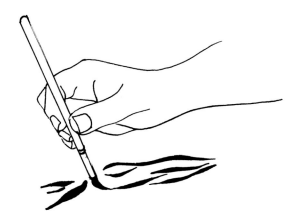

Brush Painting

The bird design below was inspired by traditional Japanese design motifs.

Bird Design

Welcome Mat

Roll out the welcome mat for new neighbors or take these cookies to a housewarming. Devour the chocolate roses, break up the cookies, and wash them down with a cup of your favorite brew.

Icing: White Modeling Chocolate, Dark Modeling Chocolate, and Meringue Powder Royal Icing ▬ pages 133, 133, and 135
Suggested Cookie: Shortbread I ▬ page 128

PROCEDURE

Follow the recipe directions for making Shortbread I. Trace the pattern and place it on the rolled-out dough. Cut carefully with an X-acto knife or use cookie cutters in similar shapes. Bake and cool the cookies according to directions. When ready to ice, make three icings, White Modeling Chocolate, Dark Modeling Chocolate, and Meringue Powder Royal Icing.

White Chocolate Rose

To make a medium-size rose, you need one white-chocolate rose base and eight petals. You'll need three medium-size roses to complete this project. First, make a base by rolling a piece of White Modeling Chocolate about 1 inch (2.5 cm) in diameter. Place the chocolate between both hands and rotate your hands in opposite directions to create a round ball shape.

If you're right-handed, put the ball of chocolate in your left hand. With your right hand, apply light pressure with your index and middle fingers as you roll the ball back and forth, creating a tip at one end. This should form a cone shape. Place the finished shape in the Cone-Shaped Rose Base pattern (page 50). The cone should fit inside the pattern.

Next, make eight marble-size balls to be flattened and shaped. Place each ball inside the Marble-Size Ball pattern (page 50) to check for size. All eight balls should fit inside the pattern.

To make the first petal, put one of the balls on your work surface. Put a piece of heavy-duty plastic wrap or a piece of Mylar or a piece of a plastic kitchen zipper bag over the ball. With your thumb, beginning at the 9 o'clock position, apply light to heavy pressure as you move your thumb from the 9 to the 3 o'clock position. Shape the ball immediately to resemble a flat round shape, with the left size of the petal being heavy and the right size being very thin.

The petal's sides should be thin. Run your thumb around the sides of the petal for thinness. Remove the plastic by pulling from the heavy side to avoid tearing the petal. Put the petal inside the Flattened Rose Petal Size (page 50); the first eight petals should fit inside circle "8."

ADDING THE FIRST PETAL

STEP 1. Make cone-shaped
rose base.

STEP 2. Flatten and
shape first rose petal.

STEP 3. Attach first petal
to the rose base.

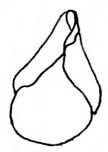

STEP 4. Wrap the petal
around the base.

Place the first petal around the cone, raising the petal about one-third higher than the tip of the cone base. The thin edge should be at the top. Wrap the petal around the cone, leaving a tiny hole at the top of the cone. The petal should only fit around the top to the middle of the cone-shaped rose base and not around the entire cone (see Adding the First Petal, above). Do not seal the edges yet.

Using the next two Flattened Rose Petal Sizes as guides (see page 50), shape the petals as you did the first petal. Once you have the correct flattened size, hold the petal by the bottom (the heavy side). Use your opposite hand and place it in back of the petal at the top center.

Beginning at the center, pinch the top slightly and move your thumb and middle finger down the sides of the ball to the middle of the ball to form a rose petal. Move your fingers back to the top to go over the petal for a more realistic look. Repeat this procedure for the next petal.

The first finished petal, remember, was placed over any seam in the cone and slightly higher than the cone (above Steps 3 and 4). Place the second petal opposite the first and slightly higher than the cone. Overlap the sides of the petals, pressing lightly. As you overlap the sides, remember to keep the integrity of the folded sides for a more natural look. Now you can seal the bottom edges of the petals. You've created a rosebud.

ADDING THE SECOND PETAL
Rosebud and Medium-Size Rose

Second Rose Petal

Rosebud
(rose base with two petals)

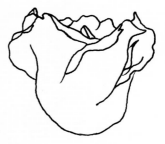

Medium-Size Rose
(eight petals)

Shape the next five petals. Attach the fourth petal over one of the seams of the rosebud. Do not seal in the edges, especially not the left side of the first petal you are attaching. Leave that side open. Attach the fifth petal, overlapping the fourth petal. The petal should overlap about one-third of the previous petal. Position the fifth petal to the right of the fourth petal, attaching it in a counterclockwise direction. Continue with the sixth and seventh petals, overlapping the previous petals. When attaching the eighth petal, overlap the seventh petal, and lift up the fourth petal (the first petal). Seal the eighth petal inside the fourth petal. Overlap the fourth petal of the eighth petal (see Rose, right bottom, page 49). You now have a medium-size bloom.

Chocolate Leaves

For leaves, color White Modeling Chocolate in a pale green shade. Roll out a piece of modeling paste as thinly as possible. Cut some leaves by hand (see Step 1 on page 51). To do this, position an X-acto knife at a 45° angle. Cut oval shapes freehand. Or use the Leaf-Shape Patterns (this page, below), if you wish.

Score the leaves by dragging lines from the top to the bottom of the leaf with a skewer or rounded toothpick. Or press the back of a clean rose leaf on the chocolate, or press a silicone leaf press on the chocolate petal for texture (Step 2).

Place the petal on a cell pad. Using a dog-bone tool, soften the edge of the petal, giving some life to the shape (see Step 3 on page 51).

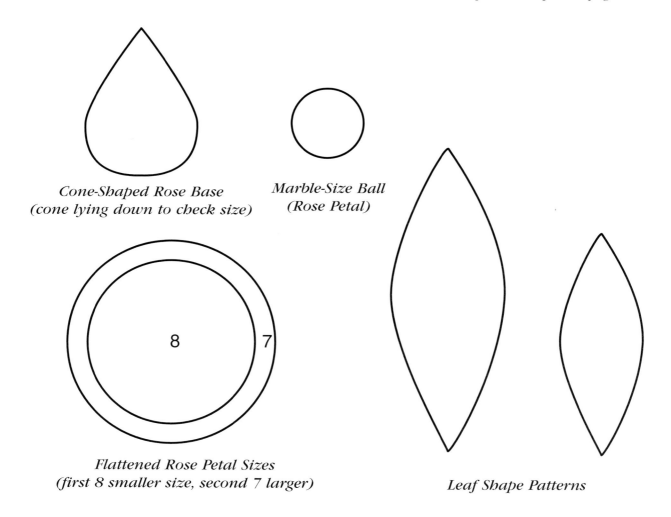

Cone-Shaped Rose Base
(cone lying down to check size)

Marble-Size Ball
(Rose Petal)

8 7

Flattened Rose Petal Sizes
(first 8 smaller size, second 7 larger)

Leaf Shape Patterns

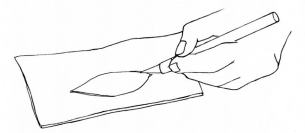

STEP 1. Cut the leaf from rolled icing with an X-acto knife.

STEP 2. (*not shown*) To create veins, use a silicone leaf press or score them with a toothpick.

STEP 3. Soften leaf with a dog-bone tool.

Marbling Technique

Roll out a piece of White Modeling Chocolate. Using pieces of dark chocolate and green Rolled Fondant, stud the White Modeling Chocolate. Roll everything as one marbled piece. Cut with a large round cutter and carefully place the marble icing on a large cookie that has been brushed with Sieved Apricot Jam.

Cookie

As soon as the cookie comes out of the oven, prepare a saucer lightly dusted with all-purpose flour. Let the cookie cool for 5 minutes. Carefully remove the large round cookie with a wide spatula. Place the cookie on the saucer and carefully press the cookie onto the plate. Let the cookie dry overnight.

The next day, remove the cookie from the saucer and place it on parchment paper (back side up). Let it dry for 12 hours. Once dried, brush the plate with Sieved Apricot Jam and ice with marbled Modeling Chocolate.

Assembly

Attach roses with Meringue Powder Royal Icing. Position roses at 11, 3, and 7 o'clock. Cut the bases of the roses on a bias so that the roses lean to one side. Place leaves between each rose with Meringue Powder Royal Icing.

Sign

Cut off some of the marbled chocolate and cover a small oval cookie. Pipe the words "Welcome Mat" by hand. Gild them with gold.

"Home Sweet Home"

This delightful cookie—sweet, homey, simple, and fun—can serve as a welcome to friends and neighbors. Make up several cookies and present them to newcomers in your neighborhood.

Icing: Glacé Icing, Rolled Fondant, and Meringue Powder Royal Icing ▢ pages 137, 131, and 135
Suggested Cookie: Lemon & Orange Cream Cookies ▢ page 125

PROCEDURE
Follow the recipe directions for making Lemon & Orange Cream Cookies. Trace the pattern (a rectangle) and place it on the rolled-out cookie dough. Cut carefully with an X-acto knife or use cookie cutters in similar shapes. Bake and cool the cookies according to directions. When ready to ice, make three icings, Glacé Icing, Rolled Fondant, and Meringue Powder Royal Icing.

Cookie
Roll out the cookie dough a little thicker than usual. After the cookie bakes and cools, let it sit for 1 hour. Then, turn the cookie on the opposite side and let dry 1 hour. This will create a firmer cookie.

Outline and flood the cookie with Glacé Icing. Let dry for 6 to 12 hours. Cut the house and banner out of Rolled Fondant. Transfer the inscription or pipe it ("Home Sweet Home") by hand.

Cut out the door and chimney from Rolled Fondant. Attach them to the house. Over-pipe the perimeter of the door and chimney with a #2 round metal piping tip. Pipe windows with a #0 metal tip.

Soften some Meringue Powder Royal Icing with a little water, or use Glacé Icing. Put the icing in a small paper cone and cut a tiny hole. Pipe Swiss dots all over the house (see page 23). Attach the house with a little water. Add plunger flowers to the cookie (see page 24).

In a book of calligraphy or typography, find lettering or a typeface you like. With a pencil, trace or copy the letters onto parchment or tracing paper. Practice piping the words on paper, using your pencil marks as a guide. Finally, pipe the words on the cookie.

House Pattern

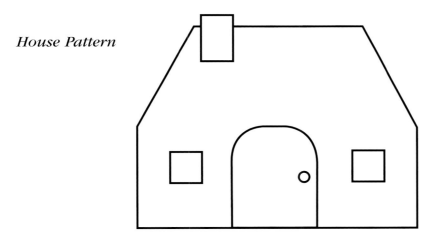

Banner Pattern

Home Sweet Home

Nautical Design

You'll want to pipe "Anchors Away" or "Bon Voyage" on these cookies. Fill a white or blue tin tied up with white and blue ribbons. Give them to departing friends, along with a bottle of fine bubbly.

Icing: Glacé Icing and Meringue Powder Royal Icing ▪ pages 137 and 135
Suggested Cookie: Butter Cookies ▪ page 124

PROCEDURE
Follow the recipe directions for making Butter Cookies. Trace the cookie pattern and place it on the rolled-out dough. Cut carefully with an X-acto knife or use cookie cutters in similar shapes. Bake and cool the cookies according to directions. When ready to ice, make two icings, Glacé Icing and Meringue Powder Royal Icing.

Anchor & Life Buoy
Outline and flood the cookies. Let them dry for 2 to 6 hours. Practice lettering and embroidery before applying it on Anchor and Life Buoy cookies. Pipe lines on the Life Buoy with a #2 round metal piping tip with Meringue Powder Royal Icing.

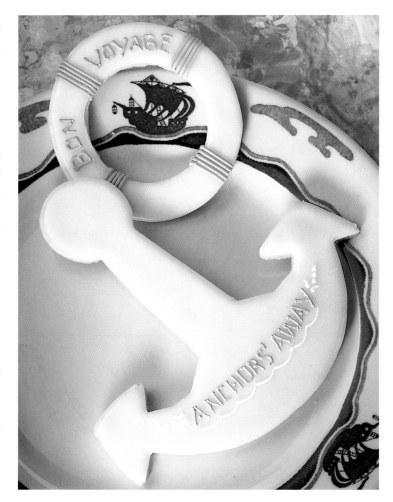

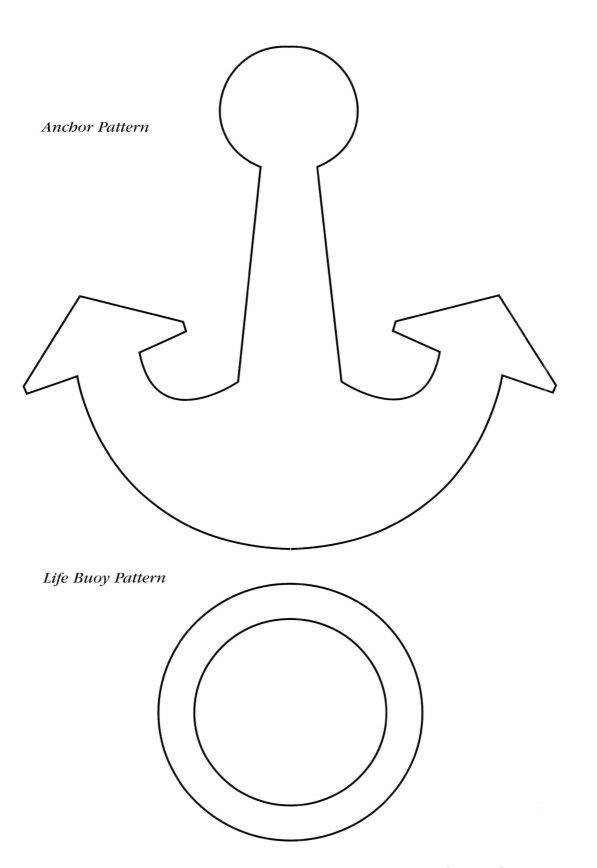

Anchor Pattern

Life Buoy Pattern

Kids' Corner

A train engine and a pretty bow make neat cookie gifts for kids. They're great for a small birthday party. Pipe each child's name on his or her own cookie.

Icing: Glacé Icing and Meringue Powder Royal Icing ▆ pages 137 and 135
Additions: Paste or Gel Food Colors and Gilding ▆ page 138
Suggested Cookie: Butter Cookies ▆ page 124

PROCEDURE
Follow the recipe directions for making Butter Cookies. Trace the pattern and place it on the rolled-out dough. Cut carefully with an X-acto knife or use cookie cutters in similar shapes. Bake and cool the cookies according to directions. When ready to ice, make two icings, Glacé Icing and Meringue Powder Royal Icing.

Train Engine
Outline and flood the entire train engine in red Glacé Icing. Let dry for 6 to 12 hours. When dried, paint the wheels black with paste or gel food coloring. Gild the front and bottom features of the engine. Pipe and gild the child's name.

Bow
Outline and flood the bow in peach, pink, lavender, or yellow. Before the icing dries, pipe some dots in white Glacé Icing, creating a polka-dot effect. Let dry for 6 to 12 hours. When dried, pipe and gild the child's name. Add a cluster of plunger flowers in the center of the bow.

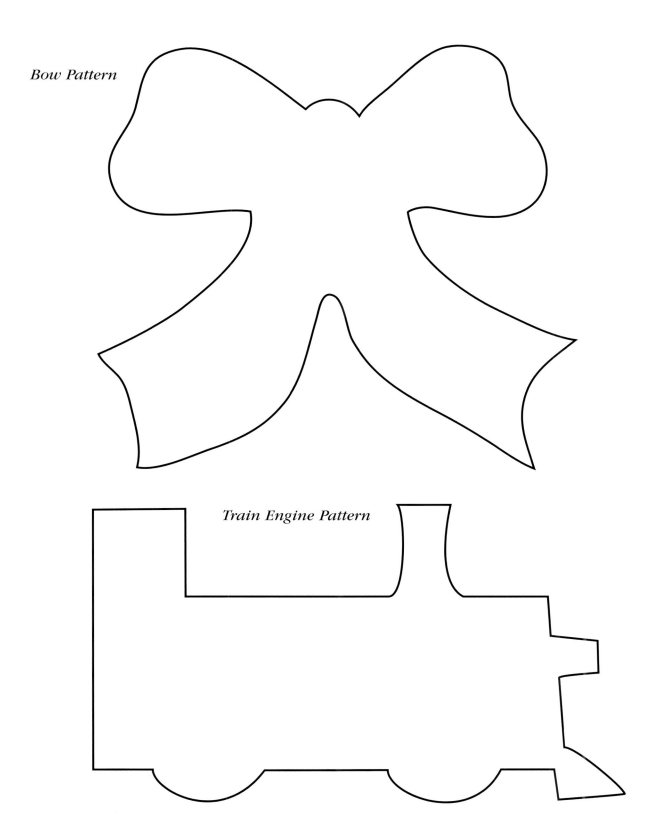

Bow Pattern

Train Engine Pattern

Gingerbread Boy & Girl

This adorable gingerbread or chocolate boy and girl make a winning duo. Outline and flood the cookies ahead of time, and let the kids decorate and outfit their own cookies.

Icing: Glacé Icing, Meringue Powder Royal Icing, Rolled Fondant ▪ pages 137, 135, and 131
Suggested Cookie: Gingerbread Cookies or Chocolate Cookies ▪ pages 130 and 127

PROCEDURE
Follow the recipe directions for making Gingerbread Cookies or Chocolate Cookies. Trace the pattern and place it on the rolled-out cookie dough. Cut carefully with an X-acto knife or use cookie cutters in similar shapes. Bake and cool the cookies according to directions. When ready to ice, make three icings, Glacé Icing, Meringue Powder Royal Icing, and Rolled Fondant.

Gingerbread Boy
Outline and flood the cookies. Let them dry for 4 to 6 hours. For the shirt, roll out a piece of Rolled Fondant. Using the same cookie cutter, cut figures out of the Rolled Fondant. Cut off the head, shorten the sleeve, and cut slightly below the stomach (see Rolled Fondant Cutouts). Stitch the neckline and all around the shirt (see "Stitching" on Shirt and Blouse, page 60). Pipe three dots for "buttons" and attach the shirt on a dried cookie with a little water (see photo page 58).

Gingerbread Girl
Outline and flood the cookies. Let dry for 4 to 6 hours. For the dress, roll out a piece of white

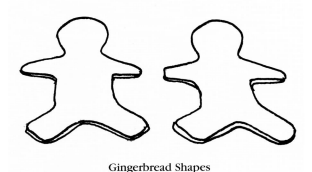

Gingerbread Shapes   Rolled Fondant Cutouts

Rolled Fondant. Using the same cookie cutter, cut figures out of the Rolled Fondant (see Gingerbread Shapes, page 59). Cut off the head, cut a lower neckline, shorten the sleeve, and cut slightly below the stomach (see Rolled Fondant Cutouts, page 59). Stitch the neckline and all around the dress, except for the bottom.

Stick tiny pieces of paper under the shoulder of the dress to give a "puffy" look. Cut a small ribbon of Rolled Fondant and slightly thin the edges. Attach the ribbon to the dress with a dot of Meringue Powder Royal Icing. Attach the dress with a little water (see Blouse below).

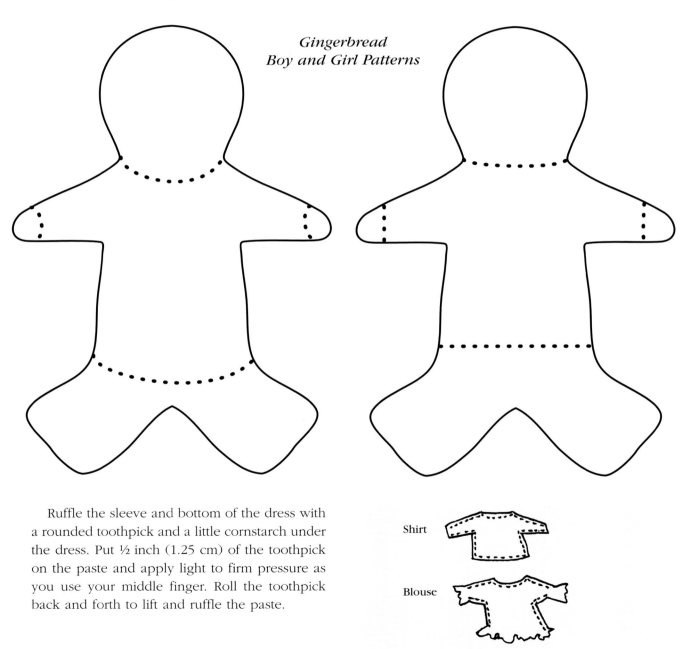

Gingerbread Boy and Girl Patterns

Shirt

Blouse

Ruffle the sleeve and bottom of the dress with a rounded toothpick and a little cornstarch under the dress. Put ½ inch (1.25 cm) of the toothpick on the paste and apply light to firm pressure as you use your middle finger. Roll the toothpick back and forth to lift and ruffle the paste.

Fruit Shapes

Eating cookies in various fruit shapes somehow seems healthful. Enjoy these with a tall glass of milk, juice, or your favorite beverage.

Icing: Glacé Icing, Meringue Powder Royal Icing, and Rolled Fondant ▬ pages 137, 135, and 131
Additions: Paste Food Colors or Gel Food Colors
Suggested Cookie: Butter Cookies or Almond Paste Cookies ▬ pages 124 and 126

PROCEDURE

Follow the recipe directions for making Butter Cookies or Almond Paste Cookies. Trace the pattern and place it on the rolled-out dough. Cut carefully with an X-acto knife or use cookie cutters in similar shapes. Bake and cool the cookies according to directions. When ready to ice, make three icings, Glacé Icing, Meringue Powder Royal Icing, and Rolled Fondant.

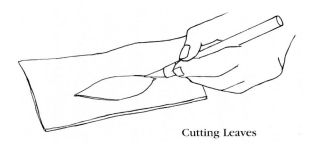

Cutting Leaves

Apple

Outline and flood with red Glacé Icing. Let dry for 2 to 6 hours. When the iced cookie is completely dry, color some Rolled Fondant green. Roll thinly and cut out a couple of leaves by hand (see Cutting Leaves). With a toothpick, slightly vein the leaves; thin the leaves' edges by hand and, using a dog-bone tool, shape them (see page 62). Attach the leaves to the top of the cookie with a little water. Color some Rolled Fondant brown. Make a small stem and attach it to the leaves and the cookie with a little water.

Pear

Outline and flood with brown and beige Glacé Icing. Don't mix the icing completely; allow streaks of brown to remain in the icing. Let dry for 2 to 6 hours. When the flood and outline icing is completely dry, color some Rolled Fondant green. Roll thinly and cut a couple of leaves by hand. Slightly vein the leaves and thin the edges of the leaves. Attach the leaves to the top of cookie with a little water. Color some Rolled Fondant brown. Make a small stem and attach it to the cookie with a little water.

Shape leaves, using a dog-bone tool.

Pear Pattern

Apple Pattern

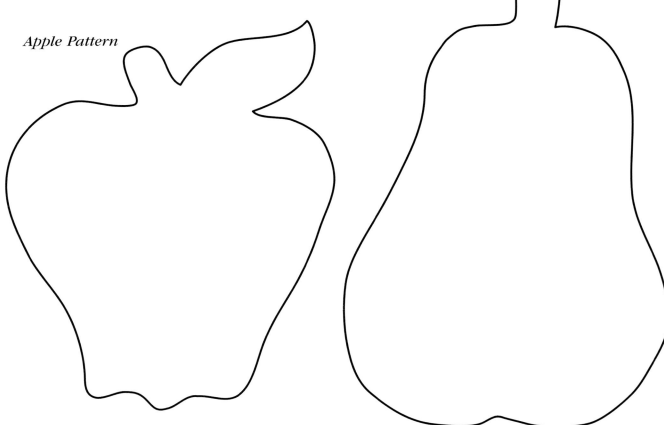

The Sampler

A sampler plate of these cookies would be a great icebreaker at any party. It's sure to please everyone who indulges.

Icing: Glacé Icing and Glacé Outline Icing ▪ pages 137 and 138
Suggested Cookie: Butter Cookies, Chocolate Cookies, Almond Paste Cookies, or Lemon & Orange Cream Cookies ▪ pages 124, 127, 126, and 125

PROCEDURE

Follow the recipe directions for making Butter Cookies, Chocolate Cookies, Almond Paste Cookies, or Lemon & Orange Cream Cookies. Trace the pattern and place it on the rolled-out dough. Cut carefully with an X-acto knife or use cookie cutters in similar shapes. Bake and cool the cookies according to directions. When ready to ice, make two icings, Glacé Icing and Glacé Outline Icing.

These cookie designs include single and double webbing (see pages 27–28), cross techniques (see pages 28 and 92), Swiss dots (see page 23), marbling (see pages 51 and 105) and freehand styles.

Music

This cookie was designed for music lovers who were visiting from Paris, hence the French word "Menuet." Of course, the American spelling is "Minuet." Call yours "Sonata," or whatever you wish.

Icing: Dark Modeling Chocolate or Chocolate Rolled Fondant, Meringue Powder Royal Icing, and Glacé Icing ▉ pages 133 or 132, 131, 135, and 137
Additions: Gilding ▉ page 138
Suggested Cookie: Chocolate Cookies or Butter Cookies ▉ pages 127 and 124

PROCEDURE

Follow the recipe directions for making Chocolate Cookies or Butter Cookies. Trace the pattern and place it on the rolled-out dough. Cut carefully with an X-acto knife or use cookie cutters in similar shapes. Bake and cool the cookies according to directions. When ready to ice, make three icings, Dark Modeling Chocolate or Chocolate Rolled Fondant, Meringue Powder Royal Icing, and Glacé Icing.

Minuet (or Menuet)

First, practice embroidery piping with a #0 metal tip. Brush the cookie with Sieved Apricot Jam. Cover the rectangular cookie with Dark Modeling Chocolate or Chocolate Rolled Fondant.

Transfer the pattern of the musical staff onto the cookie. The treble clef and base clef can be piped freehand onto a dry staff or piped on plastic wrap, dried, and attached to the musical staff when it's dry with a dot of Meringue Powder Royal Icing.

After the icing has dried, take a little Meringue Powder Royal Icing and add a drop of water to soften it lightly. Put a teaspoon of softened Meringue Powder Royal Icing into a paper cone fitted with a #1 round metal tip. Pipe dots and lines in white or black to resemble notes as indicated by the design. Once dried, gild the word "Minuet," or "Menuet" if you prefer, and the treble clef.

Eighth Note

Outline the eighth note with Meringue Powder Royal Icing. Flood the cookie with black Glacé Icing. When the icing has dried, pipe "S"-scroll embroidery on the cookie. Pipe a small staff freehand. Pipe the base clef and a couple of notes.

Musical Staff Pattern

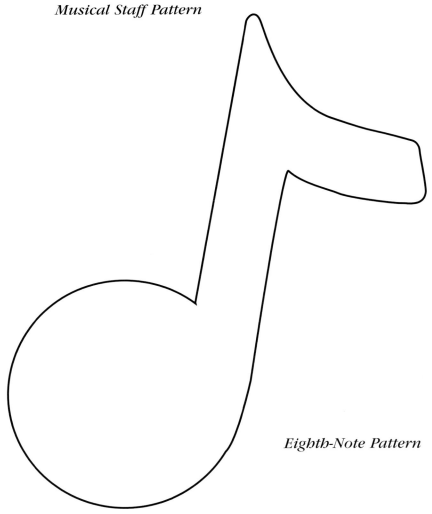

Eighth-Note Pattern

Valentine's Day

This Valentine's Day design is beautiful and timeless. Present these to your love on this special day.

Icing: Rolled Fondant, Glacé Icing, Meringue Powder Royal Icing, Dark Modeling Chocolate, and White Modeling Chocolate ▪ pages 131, 137, 135, 133, and 133
Additions: Sugar Crystals
Suggested Cookie: Shortbread I, Butter Cookies, or Chocolate Cookies ▪ pages 128, 124, and 127

PROCEDURE
Follow the recipe directions for making Shortbread I, Butter Cookies, or Chocolate Cookies. Trace the pattern and place it on the rolled-out dough. Cut carefully with an X-acto knife or use cookie cutters in similar shapes. Bake and cool the cookies according to directions. When ready to ice, make five icings, Rolled Fondant, Glacé Icing, Meringue Powder Royal Icing, Dark Modeling Chocolate, and White Modeling Chocolate.

Top Cookie
Buy a cupid-with-arrow or a similar mold from your local craft or cake-decorating store. Roll out bluish or lavender-colored fondant to ¼ inch (0.6 cm) thick.

Press the cupid mold into the Rolled Fondant. Pick-up the fondant and make sure that you have filled the entire cavity of the mold.

Extend the fondant to ensure that you have covered the mold and used enough paste to also cover the cookie. Release the mold. Use a heart-shaped cookie cutter to cut out the cookie shape. Attach the fondant cutout with Sieved Apricot Jam. Dust the edge of the cookie with lavender petal dust. Pipe loose embroidery around the edge of the cookie. Gild the arrow.

Middle Cookie
Outline the cookie with white Meringue Powder Royal Icing. Flood the cookie with red Glacé Icing. When the outline and flood icings are hard dry, pipe loose Cornelli lace around the perimeter of the cookie. For the red ball, shape a piece of White Modeling Chocolate into a round ball by first placing the chocolate in your left hand. Then use your right hand on top of the chocolate and move your hands in opposite directions. (If you're left-handed, it might be easier to place the ball in your right hand and to move your left hand on top.) Apply light to heavy pressure until you have created a round ball.

Brush the chocolate ball with light corn syrup. Roll the ball in red sugar crystals. Shake off the excess. Attach the chocolate ball to the cookie with a little Meringue Powder Royal Icing. Pipe two zigzag lines extending from the ball.

Bottom Cookie

Roll out a piece of Dark Modeling Chocolate. Roll inexpensive lace over the chocolate to create a textured look. Brush the lace with a little white vegetable shortening so that it won't stick to the chocolate. Brush the cookie with Sieved Apricot Jam. Cut out the Dark Modeling Chocolate with a large heart-shaped cookie cutter that's the same size as the cookie. Carefully place it on the cookie. Pipe loose Cornelli lace (see page 22) with some embroidery piping on the perimeter of the cookie. Cut two narrow strips of the embossed Dark Modeling Chocolate. Attach them around the edge of the cookie with light corn syrup. Gild the tops of the strips.

Roll out some White Modeling Chocolate. Cut with a smaller heart-shaped cutter. Using an X-acto knife, carefully cut the heart in half (below left). Let dry for 1 hour. Pipe loose Cornelli lace with some embroidery piping on the perimeter of the chocolate. Attach the two halves together at a 45° angle. Hold in place with a Meringue Powder Royal Icing and some rounded White Modeling Chocolate balls under the two half hearts. Make a spray of flowers out of Quick Gum Paste or purchase a ready-made spray.

Embroidery Piping

Heart Patterns

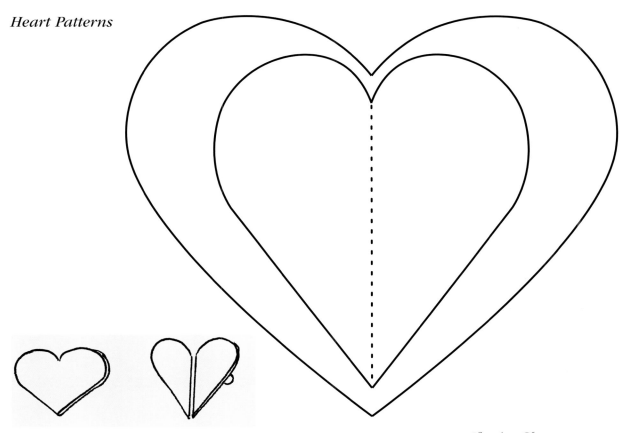

Queen of Hearts

Present these large elegant cookies at a special dinner with close friends. Give each guest a selected heart in a gift box. Serve a collection of small hearts with coffee or tea.

Icing: Glacé Icing, Meringue Powder Royal Icing, and Rolled Fondant ▪ pages 137, 135, and 131
Suggested Cookie: Almond Paste Cookies, Butter Cookies, or Chocolate Cookies ▪ pages 126, 124, and 127

PROCEDURE
Follow the recipe directions for making Almond Paste Cookies, Butter Cookies, or Chocolate Cookies. Trace the pattern and place it on the rolled-out dough. Cut carefully with an X-acto knife or use cookie cutters in similar shapes. Bake and cool the cookies according to directions. When ready to ice, make three icings, Glacé Icing, Meringue Powder Royal Icing, and Rolled Fondant.

Top & Bottom Cookies
Outline the cookies with Meringue Powder Royal Icing. Flood the cookies with Glacé Icings (use deep tones). When hard dry, pipe 3–2–1 pyramid dots on the edges of the top and bottom cookies (see Piping Pyramid Border Dots on page 72). Gild with gold.

Roll out white Rolled Fondant. Roll a piece of inexpensive lace over the icing to achieve a textured look. Brush the lace with a little white vegetable shortening so that it won't stick to the chocolate. Cut out the icing with a smaller heart-shaped cutter. Attach it to the center of the top and bottom cookies. Pipe "I Love You" on the top cookie. Pipe some fine embroidery piping on the arrow. Pipe fine embroidery on the edge of the bottom cookie.

Make two calyx flowers by cutting two small calyxes in a bluish color. Slightly pull the petals forward, using a dog-bone tool. Attach one petal inside the other with a dot of Meringue Powder Royal Icing. Pipe dots in the center for stamens. (See Calyx Flower Shaped with Dog-Bone Tool and Piping Stamen on page 72.) Attach the flower to the upper left corner of the top cookie and in the center of the bottom cookie.

Middle Cookies
Outline the cookies with Meringue Powder Royal Icing. Mix several colors of Glacé Icing and flood the cookies. When hard dry, pipe "Love" or other messages on the cookies. Gild the edges of the cookies.

Heart and Arrow Pattern

Piping Pyramid Border Dots

Simple Heart Pattern

Calyx Flower Shaped with Dog-Bone Tool

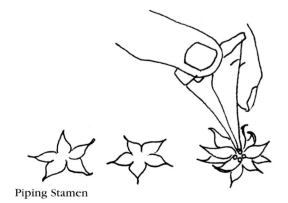

Piping Stamen

Monograms

These cookies are appropriate at wedding showers, as dessert at rehearsal dinners, and of course, they can be given, exquisitely boxed, as wedding favors.

Icing: White Modeling Chocolate, Dark Modeling Chocolate, Glacé Icing, Glacé Outline Icing, and Meringue Powder Royal Icing ▬ pages 133, 133, 137, 138, and 135
Suggested Cookie: Butter Cookies, Chocolate Cookies, or Almond Paste Cookies ▬ pages 124, 127, and 126

PROCEDURE
Follow the recipe directions for making Butter Cookies, Chocolate Cookies, or Almond Paste Cookies. Trace the pattern and place it on the rolled-out dough. Cut carefully with an X-acto knife or use cookie cutters in similar shapes. (A scalloped-oval cookie pattern is on page 99.) Bake and cool the cookies according to directions. When ready to ice, make five icings, White Modeling Chocolate, Dark Modeling Chocolate, Glacé Icing, Glacé Outline Icing, and Meringue Powder Royal Icing.

For a transparent outline look, outline the cookies with Glacé Outline Icing. Flood the cookies with Glacé Icing. When dry, the outline will blend into the Glacé Icing. Let the cookies dry for 2 to 4 hours for surface drying or 6 to 12 hours for hard drying.

Oval Shape
First, outline and flood the cookie in Glacé Icing. Let the cookies dry for 2 to 4 hours. Then, outline and flood the letter "G" or another initial in Meringue Powder Flood Icing. When the icing is dry (2 to 4 hours), slide an offset spatula under the monogram and carefully place it on the oval-shaped iced cookie with a dot of Meringue Powder Royal Icing. Practice the embroidery first; then pipe them on the cookie by hand.

Heart Shape
First outline and flood the heart-shaped cookie with Glacé Icing. When it is dry, carbon-copy or pipe the "M E" monogram (or one more appropriate for your recipients) freehand on the heart-shaped iced cookie. Pipe over the carbon-copy design with nut-brown Meringue Powder Royal Icing, using a #2 round metal piping tip. Practice embroidery piping first; then pipe on the cookie freehand.

Scalloped Oval
First, brush the cookie with Sieved Apricot Jam. Then roll out the Dark Modeling Chocolate. Cover the cookie. Roll out the White Modeling

Chocolate and cut with a smaller oval cutter. Pinprick the monograms "A P S" (or initials appropriate for your recipients) and outline with nut-brown Meringue Powder Royal Icing. Gild with gold.

Letter "G"

Outline the cookie with Glacé Outline Icing. Then flood it with Glacé Icing. When the icing on the cookie is dry, pipe freehand embroidery. Attach some plunger flowers (see page 24) to finish the design with dots of Meringue Powder Royal Icing.

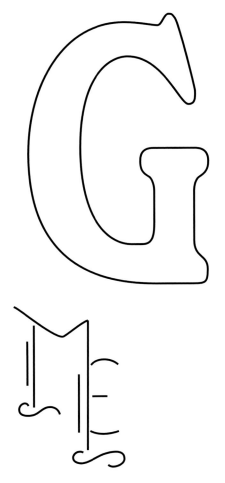

Monogram Patterns

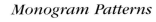

High Table Wedding Design

These ornately decorated cookies belong on the high table at a wedding. Present them, exquisitely boxed and trimmed with lovely ribbons, to the parents and anyone of honor at the high table.

Icing: Meringue Powder Royal Icing, Rolled Fondant, and Dark Modeling Chocolate pages 135, 131, and 133
Additions: Spray of Gum-Paste Flowers
Suggested Cookie: Butter Cookies or Shortbread I pages 124 and 128

PROCEDURE

Follow the recipe directions for making Butter Cookies or Shortbread I. Trace the pattern and place it on the rolled-out dough. Cut carefully with an X-acto knife or use cookie cutters in similar shapes. Bake and cool the cookies according to directions. When you're ready to ice, make three icings, Meringue Powder Royal Icing, Rolled Fondant, and Dark Modeling Chocolate.

Bell

Brush the cookie with Sieved Apricot Jam. Roll fondant to ⅛ inch (0.3 cm) thick. Cut and carefully place it on the cookie. Stitch the perimeter with a quilting tool if you wish, or emboss with an embroidery stamp near the perimeter.

Place the iced cookie on a board covered with decorative foil. Secure it with Meringue Powder Royal Icing. For an added dimension, pipe an out-line around the cookie about ⅛ inch (0.3 cm) from the cookie. Flood with Meringue Powder Flood Icing or Glacé Icing. To achieve an even larger look, pipe another perimeter around the flood design. Place a spray of handmade or bought gum-paste (recipe page 139) flowers on the cookie.

Note: You can replace the gum-paste flowers with a piped, flooded, and gilded monogram.

Double-Heart Cookie

Brush the two cookies with Sieved Apricot Jam. Attach both cookies together, with the smaller heart in the center of the larger heart, with Meringue Powder Royal Icing. Roll Dark Modeling Chocolate to ⅛ inch (0.3 cm) thick. Cut the chocolate with the larger heart pattern or cutter. Cover both cookies as one sandwich cookie, stretching the chocolate slightly to fit over the sides of both. Emboss the perimeter of the larger cookie with embossing stamps. Create a beautiful chocolate rose and leaves with the edge of the rose gilded.

Note: You can replace the chocolate rose with an outlined, flooded, and gilded monogram.

Chocolate Rose

To make a full-size chocolate rose, you need one chocolate base and 15 petals. Follow the same procedure as for making medium-size roses in the Welcome Mat cookies (pages 47–50).

For a full bloom, take a medium-size rose and make seven more petals. Start at any one of the seams (where two petals overlap). Attach the petals as you did in petals 4 through 8. Each layer of petals should be slightly higher than the previous one. Thus, after creating petals 2 and 3, petals 4 through 8 should be slightly higher than the rosebud. Petals 9 through 15 should be slightly higher than the medium bloom.

Chocolate Leaves

Roll out a piece of Dark Modeling Chocolate. Roll it out as thinly as possible. Cut out some leaves by hand. Give the leaves veins by using the back of a washed and dried rose leaf or use a silicone leaf press. Soften the edges of the leaves with a dog-bone tool for a realistic and natural look (see drawings on page 51).

Position the leaves on the iced cookie. Overlap the leaves using a damp paintbrush. Place the rose in the center of the cookie with a few dots of Meringue Powder Royal Icing.

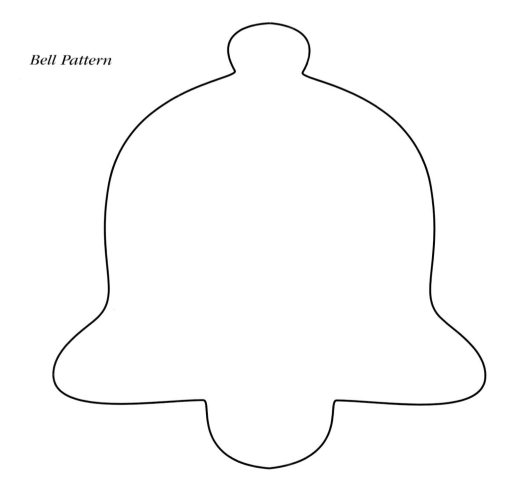

Bell Pattern

Wedding Cake Cookies

These elegant cookies shaped like a wedding cake make great favors for wedding guests. Or use them as small thank-you gifts for the best man, maid of honor, bridesmaids, and ushers.

Icing: Glacé Icing, Egg White Royal Icing, Meringue Powder Royal Icing, and Rolled Fondant ▮ pages 137, 134, 135, and 131
Additions: Paste Food Colors and Gel Food Colors
Suggested Cookie: Butter Cookies or Shortbread I ▮ pages 124 and 128

PROCEDURE

Follow the recipe directions for making Butter Cookies or Shortbread I. Trace the pattern and place it on the rolled-out dough. Cut carefully with an X-acto knife or use cookie cutters in similar shapes. Bake and cool the cookies according to directions. When ready to ice, make four icings, Glacé Icing, Egg White Royal Icing, Meringue Powder Royal Icing, and Rolled Fondant.

Monogrammed Cookie

Outline and flood the cookie with white Glacé Icing. Let dry for 6 to 12 hours. For the center, color some Rolled Fondant with peach color. Roll out a small piece and cut out a scalloped oval shape. Let it dry for 2 hours. When it has dried, pipe a monogram. Attach it to the center of the Wedding Cake Cookie. Pipe Cornelli lace around the bottom of the oval shape.

For ribbons, roll out a piece of white Rolled Fondant. Cut two thin strips. Carefully soften the edge with a dog-bone tool (see Softening Ribbons). Attach it to the top of the cookie with a dot of Meringue Powder Royal Icing. Twist the ribbon to fall to the sides. Attach rosettes and leaves. Pipe an oval border with a #3 round metal piping tip (see pages 23 and 80).

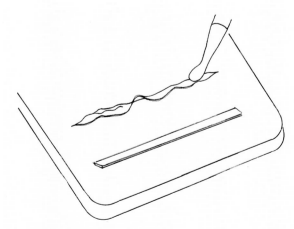

Softening Ribbons

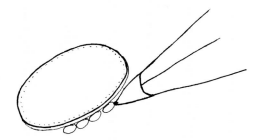

Piping an Oval Border

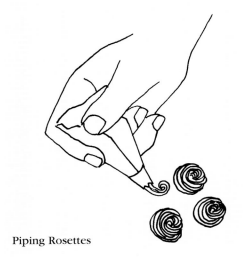

Piping Rosettes

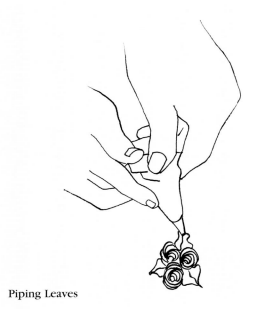

Piping Leaves

Rosettes

Prepare a flat surface with plastic wrap tightly fitted and taped with masking tape. Prepare half a recipe for Meringue Powder Royal Icing. Divide the icing into three bowls. Color two bowls of icing with paste or gel food coloring. The colors should be pale pastels. Color the third bowl with pale green icing for the leaves.

Prepare two medium-large paper cones with a #18 star-shaped tip in each bag. Half-fill the bags with the prepared and colored Meringue Powder Royal Icing. Hold the bag at a 90° angle. If you're right-handed, position the tip at 9 o'clock. If you're left-handed, position the tip at 3 o'clock. Raise the tip slightly from the prepared surface and squeeze with medium to heavy pressure. Pipe a complete circle, beginning and ending at the same spot. Right-handed people should pipe counterclockwise. Left-handed people should pipe clockwise (see Piping Rosettes).

The rotation should be tight, with no holes in the center of the flower. Stop the pressure and gently move the tip continuously to the right or left, touching the surface of the flower so that you do not to leave an exit point. Make two dozen rosettes, alternating colors. Leave space on the prepared surface for the leaves.

Leaves

Fill a medium-size paper cone with a #67 leaf tip and 1 tablespoon pale green Meringue Powder Royal Icing mixed with ½ teaspoon of water to soften the icing. Position the tip at a 45° angle. Squeeze with firm pressure and build up the front of the leaf first; then pull slightly as you ease off pressure (see Piping Leaves). Stop the pressure and pull the bag toward you.

The leaf should have a pointed tip. If you don't have a point, add a few more drops of water in the icing to soften it slightly. Make as many leaves as you wish. After they dry, remove the leaves from the paper and secure them to the rosettes with a dot of Meringue Powder Royal Icing.

Extension-Work Cookie

This cookie is decorated in the classic Australian style known as bridge and extension work. Little lines of string work are piped through a #0 metal tip extending from the middle third of the cookie to a "bridge" at the bottom of the cookie, creating a kind of lacy skirt.

To achieve this, roll out some white or peach-colored Rolled Fondant about ⅛ inch (0.3 cm) thick. Cut out the fondant with a similar type of cutter or trace and place the pattern on the fondant. Brush the cookie with Sieved Apricot Jam and attach the fondant to the cookie.

Score the top of the bottom tier with a quilting tool so that you'll have a guide for the extension (or string) work. Measure the bottom of the cookie with a ruler from left to right. Divide it into four sections.

The Bridge

Make a recipe of Egg White Royal Icing (with pasteurized egg whites). Fit a #3 round metal tip with a small amount of Egg White Royal Icing. Pipe four scallops from left to right.

Repeat by over-piping each line with the #3 metal tip. After two lines each, let them dry for 15 minutes. Repeat by piping two more lines on top of the previous lines. Let them dry for 15 minutes. Pipe a final fifth line. The line should protrude from the bottom (see Bridge Work below). This is the bridge.

Extensions or Strings

Sieve a small amount of Egg White Royal Icing through a nylon stocking or use a metal offset spatula to smash the icing against a flat surface to get rid of any lumps of sugar. Cut a small paper cone and fit it with a #0 metal tip. Add up to 1 tablespoon of Egg White Royal Icing to the bag and close.

Starting at the top of the scored line, position the metal piping tip at the top of the line and touch the cookie. Apply a burst of pressure as you begin, creating a dot; then squeeze and pull the tip upward, estimating the distance from the top of the line to the bottom of the bridge. Hold the string for a brief moment to slightly air-dry the icing. Then bring the piping tip to the bottom of the bridge and break off at the bridge or move the piping tip slightly under the bridge to break off the icing.

The next line should be between ¹⁄₁₆ and ⅛ inch (0.15 and 0.3 cm). Continue until you have completed the string work (see Extension or String Work below).

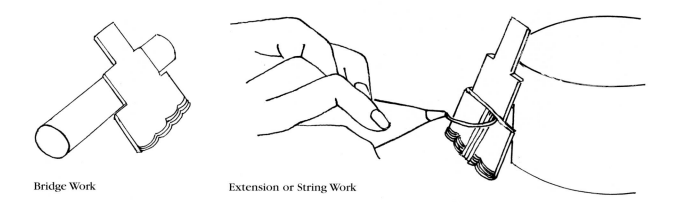

Bridge Work   Extension or String Work

Hail Spotting

This design is optional and requires a little soft-ened Egg White Royal Icing. To soften the icing, use about 1½ tablespoons of Egg White Royal Icing and about 1 teaspoon of pasteurized whites.

Put 1 teaspoon of icing in a bag. Carefully cut the very tip of the bag. Position the tip at the top of the string work and squeeze, letting the icing, and not the bag, touch the string work. Carefully space the dots on the string. Do this to every other string or every three strings.

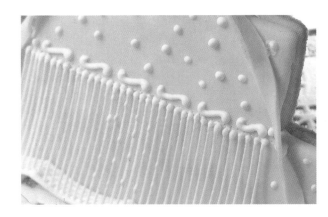

Hail spotting gives string work a lacy look.

Wedding Cake Pattern

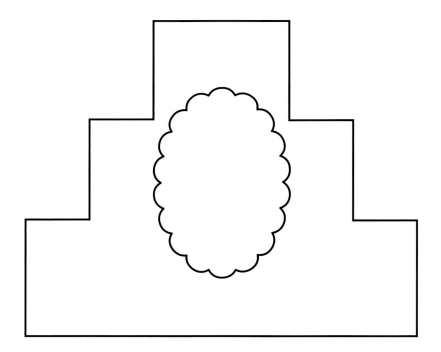

Groom's Cookies

These Groom's Cookies can be used as wedding favors in place of a groom's cake. Box them and give them out at the end of the reception. Enlarged versions can be a very special gift for a birthday.

Icing: Rolled Fondant, Meringue Powder Royal Icing, and Glacé Icing ▬ pages 131, 135, and 137
Additions: Quick Gum Paste ▬ page 139
Suggested Cookie: Chocolate Cookies or Butter Cookies ▬ pages 127 and 124

PROCEDURE

Follow the recipe directions for making Chocolate Cookies and Butter Cookies. Trace the pattern and place it on the rolled-out dough. Cut carefully with an X-acto knife or use cookie cutters in similar shapes. Bake and cool the cookies according to directions. When ready to ice, make three icings, Rolled Fondant, Meringue Powder Royal Icing, and Glacé Icing.

Color small amounts of Rolled Fondant in blue-gray, blue-black, and pink. Wrap in plastic wrap until ready to use. Make a recipe of Quick Gum Paste. Lightly brush the cookies with Sieved Apricot Jam or light corn syrup.

Quilting the Cookie

Roll out colored icing to ⅛ to ¼ inch (0.3 to 0.6 cm) thick. Roll it into a rectangular shape. Cut and trim the icing using a ruler and an X-acto knife. Using a quilting or dressmaker's tool, score lines ⅛ inch (0.3 cm) apart from top to bottom. Place the pattern on the icing and carefully cut out the designs, using an X-acto knife. If using a cutter, place the cutter on the icing and cut out as many shapes as possible. If more cookies are desired, re-roll the dough and cut. Place the cut icing directly on top of the cookies. Press carefully so that you do not destroy or disfigure scored lines.

Necktie

Trace the necktie pattern. Secure the pattern to a solid surface. Cover it with plastic wrap and tape the ends securely. Outline the necktie with Meringue Powder Royal Icing. Flood the necktie with Meringue Powder Flood Icing (for a flat look) or with Glacé Icing (for a shiny look). Immediately after flooding the necktie, pipe dots with flood icing in contrasting colors, allowing the icing to settle into the design. For a raised element in the design, allow the icing to set for 20 to 30 minutes. Pipe dots with a slightly stiffer icing or roll tiny balls of rolled icing and place them on the cookie with a dot of Meringue Powder Royal Icing.

Let the flooded necktie dry for 2 to 4 hours (for surface dry) or 6 to 12 hours (for hard dry). Carefully remove the flooded necktie cookie from the paper with an offset metal spatula and place it on the Rolled-Icing cookie with dots of Meringue Powder Royal Icing. Pipe "Dad" in Meringue Powder Royal Icing. Let this dry for 30 minutes. Gild with gold.

Loose Tie

Take a small piece of Quick Gum Paste or Rolled Fondant and roll it very thin. Cut out a small strip, about 2 inches (5 cm) long and ⅛ inch (0.3 cm) wide. Soften the strip with a dog-bone tool and cell pad. Fold the strip in half and attach it to the top of the shield cookie with a dot of Meringue Powder Royal Icing (see Top Hat & Loose Tie below).

Top Hat

Roll a rectangular piece of Quick Gum Paste very thin—about 3 inches long and 2 inches wide. Cut a strip approximately 2⅝ inches (6.5 cm) long and ½ inch (1.25 cm) wide. Trim to specifications. Use water to join the sides of the strip to form a cylinder. The piece can be slightly overlapped. Cut out the crown with another piece of paste, using the wide opening of a #2 round metal piping tip. Brush it with water and attach a cylinder directly on top (see Top Hat & Loose Tie). Trim it with an X-acto knife for a neat finish. Cut out the brim with a slightly larger cutter or pattern. Allow the icing to dry for 15 minutes.

Attach the cylinder with the crown set slightly toward the back of the brim with a water-dampened paintbrush. Let it dry. Attach with Meringue Powder Royal Icing on top of the loose tie.

Tuxedo

Cut out the vest and score it with a quilting tool. Attach the vest to the shirt with water. Cut out buttons with a #7 round metal piping tip (small end). Attach them to the tuxedo with dots of Meringue Powder Royal Icing.

Bow Tie

Cut out the bow tie using the pattern. Join the ends together to meet in the center. Attach the tie with water or dots of Meringue Powder Royal Icing. Take a tiny piece of Quick Gum Paste and roll it into a tiny ball. Place the ball in the center of the seam of the bow tie with a dot of Meringue Powder Royal Icing. (See Bow Tie below.)

Place the bow tie on top of the tuxedo shirt with a dot of Meringue Powder Royal Icing.

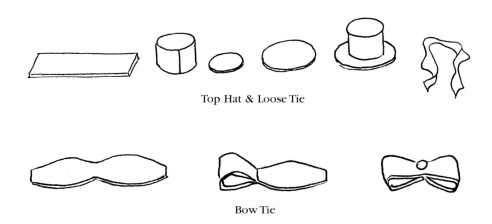

Top Hat & Loose Tie

Bow Tie

Bow-Tie Pattern

Tuxedo Jacket Pattern

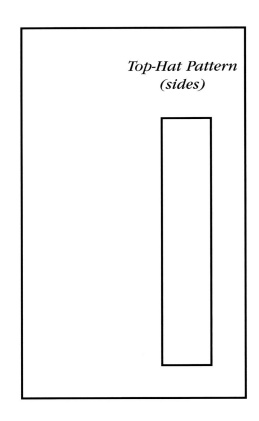

Top-Hat Pattern (sides)

Rectangle Cookie Pattern

Tuxedo Shirt Pattern

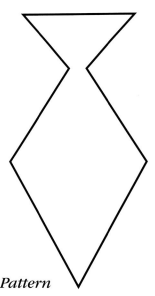

Tie Pattern

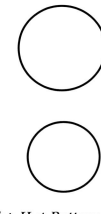

Top-Hat Patterns (crown and brim)

50th Anniversary

On their 50th anniversary, you'll want to give a timeless, elegant gift that represents 50 years of the couple's love and devotion. These cookies are a stunning tribute.

Icing: Glacé Icing, Meringue Powder Royal Icing, Dark Modeling Chocolate, and Rolled Fondant ▪ pages 137, 135, 133, and 131
Suggested Cookie: Shortbread I or Chocolate Cookies ▪ pages 128 and 127

PROCEDURE

Follow the recipe directions for making Shortbread I or Chocolate Cookies. Trace the pattern and place it on the rolled-out dough. Cut carefully with an X-acto knife or use cookie cutters in similar shapes. Bake and cool the cookies according to directions. When ready to ice, make four icings, Glacé Icing, Meringue Powder Royal Icing, Dark Modeling Chocolate, and Rolled Fondant.

Cookies

Brush the top cookie with Sieved Apricot Jam. Roll out peach- or lavender-colored Rolled Fondant to ⅛ inch (0.3 cm) thick. Cut the fondant with a cookie cutter or pattern and place it on the cookie. Pipe pretty embroidery and Swiss dots, leaving space for the monogram.

Brush the bottom cookie with Sieved Apricot Jam. Roll out the Dark Modeling Chocolate to ⅛ inch (0.3 cm) thick, cut with a cookie cutter or pattern, and carefully place it on the cookie. Emboss the edges with entwined hearts or embroidery piping. Gild the cookie's sides. For a shiny look, brush a little light corn syrup (diluted with a few drops of warm water) on top.

Monogram

Outline and flood the numbers and let them dry on clear plastic wrap taped to a hard surface (about 4 to 6 hours). When they have dried, gild the numbers. Carefully remove the numbers from plastic wrap by running a small metal offset spatula under them. Attach them to the top cookie with a drop of White Meringue Royal Icing. Cut ribbon streamers from Rolled Fondant, soften the edges, and attach them to the top of the cookie.

Easter

Adorn your Easter basket with these pretty and delectable edibles.
They'll be a treasured holiday treat.

Icing: Glacé Icing, Meringue Powder Royal Icing, Rolled Fondant, and White Modeling Chocolate ▬ pages 137, 135, 131, and 133
Additions: Liquid Whitener and Sieved Apricot Jam ▬ page 139
Suggested Cookie: Butter Cookies or Shortbread II ▬ pages 124 and 129

PROCEDURE

Follow the recipe directions for making Butter Cookies or Shortbread II. Trace the pattern and place it on the rolled-out dough. Cut carefully with an X-acto knife or use cookie cutters in similar shapes. Bake and cool the cookies according to directions. When ready to ice, make four icings, Glacé Icing, Meringue Powder Royal Icing, Rolled Fondant, and White Modeling Chocolate.

Easter Eggs

Outline the cookies with Meringue Powder Royal Icing. Pipe wavy lines in the center of one, zigzags in the center of another, diagonal lines on one, and scalloped lines on another.

It is important to touch the outline icing when piping from left to right. Make several colors of Glacé Icing.

On two of the cookies, flood one half of the cookie using one color and flood the other half with several colors, using single-web or double-web techniques (see webbing techniques on pages 27–28).

Easter Bunny

Brush the cookie with Sieved Apricot Jam and ice the bunny with tinted White Modeling Chocolate or tinted Rolled Fondant. Carefully cut and place the icing over the cookie. Roll out white Rolled Fondant.

Transfer the pattern of the raised stomach and the ears to white Rolled Fondant. Cut carefully. Brush the area with light corn syrup and carefully apply the items. Let this dry for 1 hour.

Place the pattern over the iced cookie and transfer the eyes, nose, and mouth pattern. Outline the eye areas with brown Meringue Powder Royal Icing. Outline the nose with brown Meringue Powder Royal Icing. Paint in the mouth with brown food coloring.

Flood the eyes with black or very dark brown Meringue Powder Royal Icing. Pipe (eye) pupils with white Meringue Powder Royal Icing. Flood the nose with red Glacé Icing.

Dust the ears with pink petal dust. Paint the outline of the ears with liquid whitener. Paint the outline of the eyes with liquid whitener. Dust the entire bunny with a light brown (use brown petal dust mixed with corn starch) or use a peach color.

Easter Bonnet

Brush the scalloped cookie with Sieved Apricot Jam. Place a ball of White Modeling Chocolate in the center of the cookie. Roll out a piece of colored Rolled Fondant or use tinted White Modeling Chocolate. Place a piece of lace over the icing and roll over the lace to achieve a textured pattern. Cut out the icing with a scalloped round cookie cutter (or use the pattern on page 29). Place over the cookie and shape the hat. Cut a small strip of fondant to tie over the brim of the hat. Place a few fondant flowers in a cluster to finish the hat.

Bunny Pattern

This bunny was inspired by an American Greetings card.

Christmas

*Besides the tree, presents, and laughter of children, nothing brings
holiday cheer more than hand-decorated Christmas cookies.
Why not give your relatives and friends a festive box of them?*

Icings: Glacé Icing, Meringue Powder Flood Icing, and Meringue Powder Royal Icing pages 137, 136, and 135
Suggested Cookie: Butter Cookies, Almond Paste Cookies, Chocolate Cookies, or Shortbread I pages 124, 126, 127, and 128

PROCEDURE

Follow the recipe directions for making Butter Cookies, Almond Paste Cookies, Chocolate Cookies, or Shortbread I. Trace the pattern and place it on the rolled-out dough. Cut the pattern carefully with an X-acto knife or buy cookie cutters in similar shapes. Bake and cool the cookies according to directions. When ready to ice, make three icings, Glacé Icing, Meringue Powder Flood Icing, and Meringue Powder Royal Icing.

Stars

Outline and flood the cookies with Glacé Icing or Meringue Powder Flood Icing. After they dry, over-pipe the outline icing using red or green Meringue Powder Royal Icing.

For the first star, pipe a cluster of three dots in red and green sporadically around the center of the cookie.

Make a calyx flower by cutting a small and a medium calyx in white. Slightly pull the petals forward by applying light pressure at the tip of the petal and pulling toward the center of the flower, using a dog-bone tool (see page 72).

Attach the small calyx petal inside the larger calyx. Pipe a cluster of red dots in Meringue Powder Royal Icing. Pipe a green dot in the center of the cluster. Attach the flower to the center of the cookie with icing.

For the second star, pipe lines from each apex to the center of the cookie. Pipe short lines on opposite sides of the centered line. Over-pipe lines in red and green Glacé Icings.

Brush the center of the cookie with corn syrup. Press silver dragées in the center of the cookie. Brush off any excess. Using a fine sable paintbrush, brush sections of the cookie with corn syrup. Press dragées in each brushed space.

Large Bell

Outline and flood the bell with Glacé Icing. Pipe strips of white, green, and red icing. Move the toothpick back and forth to create a web design.

Small Bell

Outline the bell; then pipe a ring close to the outline of the cookie in white Glacé Icing. Pipe the next color inside the white ring with green icing. Then follow with red icing and finally, pipe yellow icing into the center.

   Start at the center and drag a toothpick or skewer to 12 o'clock (see Cross Technique below).   Remove the toothpick and position it back at the center. Then drag a toothpick to 3 o'clock. Continue to place it back at the center, and then drag it to 6 o'clock and to 9 o'clock (Step 1). Then drag  the toothpick from the outside edge between the points, i.e., 2, 5, 7, and 11 o'clock (Step 2). This is the cross technique.

Candy Cane I

Outline and flood the cookie with Glacé Icing or Meringue Powder Flood Icing. After the icing dries, pipe red Glacé Icing in a zigzag motion from a paper cone (with a small opening). Before it sets, pipe yellow Glacé Icing in the open spaces around the zigzag design. Finally, pipe green dots in the center of the yellow Glacé Icing.

Candy Cane II

Outline and flood the cookie with Glacé Icing or Meringue Powder Flood Icing. After the icing dries, pipe red parallel lines using Glacé Icing. Pipe green dots between the parallel lines.

Christmas Tree

Outline and flood the cookie. Before the icing sets, pipe red Meringue Powder Royal Icing in a red zigzag line from the top and stream down to the bottom. To do this, position the tip at a 45° angle. Squeeze the bag and lift up the bag about 1 inch (2.5 cm) from the surface. Move your hands from right to left, putting your hands down once you reach the sides of the tree (see Piping Christmas Tree Garland on page 93). Then pipe red and yellow dots with Glacé Icing for tree ornaments.

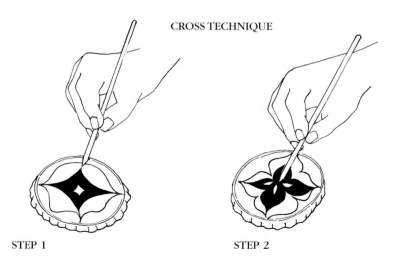

CROSS TECHNIQUE

STEP 1   STEP 2

Piping Christmas Tree Garland

Snowman

Outline and flood the snowman or, if you prefer, a snowwoman. After the icing has completely dried, paint in the hat with black paste or gel food coloring, using a medium sable brush. Outline the eyes with brown Meringue Powder Royal Icing. Flood them with black Glacé Icing. Outline the mouth and fill it in with red Glacé Icing. Pipe dots for the buttons and flood the scarf with black Glacé Icing. Attach a silver dragée with Meringue Powder Royal Icing. Pipe in white icing for the iris and pipe white polka dots on the hat.

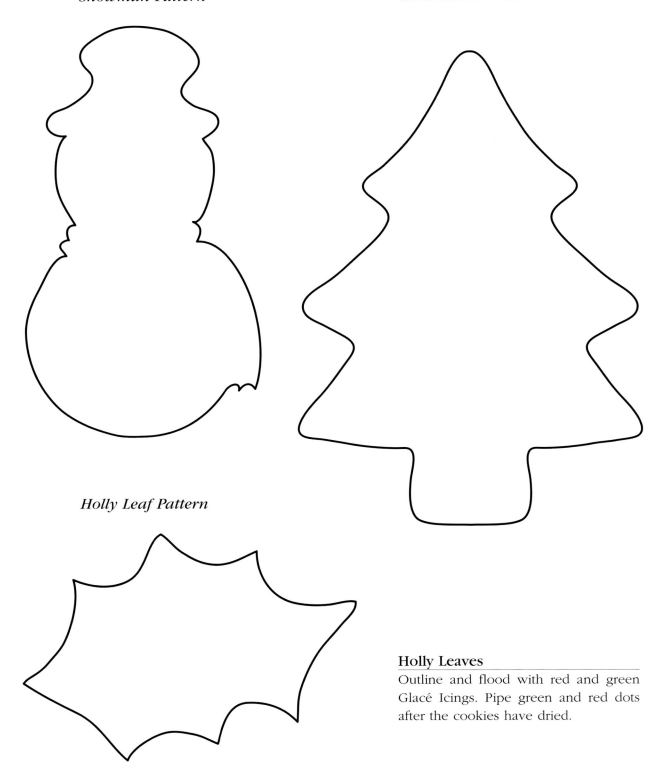

Snowman Pattern

Christmas Tree Pattern

Holly Leaf Pattern

Holly Leaves

Outline and flood with red and green Glacé Icings. Pipe green and red dots after the cookies have dried.

New Year's Eve

Here's a splendid way to bring in the New Year with a wonderful gift to present to the party-giver. Or simply enjoy these cookies with someone special along with a tall glass of champagne.

Icing: Rolled Fondant, Meringue Powder Royal Icing, and Meringue Powder Flood Icing pages 131, 135, and 136
Suggested Cookie: Almond Paste Cookies or Shortbread I pages 126 and 128

PROCEDURE

Follow the recipe directions for making Almond Paste Cookies or Shortbread I. Trace the pattern and place it on the rolled-out dough. Cut carefully with an X-acto knife or use cookie cutters in similar shapes. Bake and cool the cookies according to directions. When ready to ice, make three icings, Rolled Fondant, Meringue Powder Royal Icing, and Meringue Powder Flood Icing.

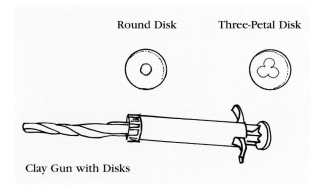

Round Disk   Three-Petal Disk

Clay Gun with Disks

Preparation

Outline enough numbers to make a clock in white Meringue Powder Royal Icing and flood them in black Meringue Powder Flood Icing. Note that you'll need to flood five "1"s, two "2"s, and one each of the remaining numbers. Outline both arrows in white icing and flood them in black. After they dry, gild the outline of the arrows.

Roll out a piece of Rolled Fondant that's large enough to cover the cookie. Cut it with a large round cookie cutter or pattern. Let it dry for 1 hour. Trace the pattern and fit it over the fondant. Pinprick or trace clock lines. Remove the pattern and score with a quilting tool. Brush the cookie with Sieved Apricot Jam and carefully place the scored fondant over the cookie.

Assembly

Place the cookie on iced or foil-covered cardboard for presentation. To do this, buy a piece of round cardboard that's a little larger than the cookie. Brush the board lightly with light corn syrup. Roll out some fondant and cut it with a cookie cutter that's the same size as the board. Carefully place the fondant on the board. Let it dry for several hours before attaching the cookie.

To make the rope design, roll out a piece of white Rolled Fondant. Knead a little white vegetable shortening into the fondant to prevent sticking. Shape it into a narrow sausage. Push the Rolled Fondant through a clay gun fitted with a three-petal disk. Gently twist the fondant as it protrudes through the clay gun (see Clay Gun on page 95). Place the rope around the perimeter of the cookie and glue it on with water or dots of Meringue Powder Royal Icing.

After the numbers have dried and have been gilded, place them on the appropriate quilted line, glued with dots of Meringue Powder Royal Icing. Use the clay gun fitted with a round disk to place a strip of ivory-colored Rolled Fondant inside the rope. Attach Rolled Fondant plunger flowers at each seam. Decorate the perimeter of the cardboard with scroll piping.

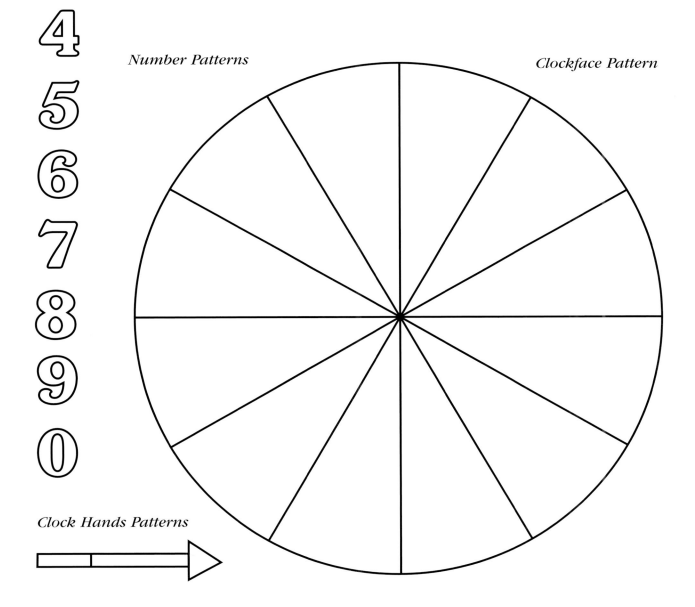

Number Patterns

Clockface Pattern

Clock Hands Patterns

Stained Glass

This stained-glass design is appropriate for an art gallery opening, church gathering, garden party, or private dinner for a select few.

Icing: White Modeling Chocolate, Rolled Fondant, and Meringue Powder Royal Icing ▬ pages 133, 131, and 135
Additions: Piping Gel
Suggested Cookie: Lemon & Orange Cream Cookies ▬ page 125

PROCEDURE
Follow the recipe directions for making Lemon & Orange Cream Cookies. Trace the pattern and place it on the rolled-out dough. Cut carefully with an X-acto knife or use cookie cutters in similar shapes. Bake and cool the cookies according to directions. When ready to ice, make three icings, White Modeling Chocolate, Rolled Fondant, and Meringue Powder Royal Icing.

Brush the cookies with Sieved Apricot Jam. Roll and cut the icing. Carefully place the icing on the cookies. Trim with an X-acto knife for a neat finish. (**Hint**: Carefully turn the cookie and icing over and trim with the bottom of the cookie facing up.) Trace the pattern and transfer it onto the cookies. Use the pinprick method to transfer the designs.

Buy piping gel from your local cake-decorating store. Outline the pattern on the cook-

ies with brown-colored Meringue Powder Royal Icing, using a #2 round piping tip. Color small amounts of piping gel in green, yellow, and deep pink. Fill small parchment cones with the colors.

Stained-Glass Patterns

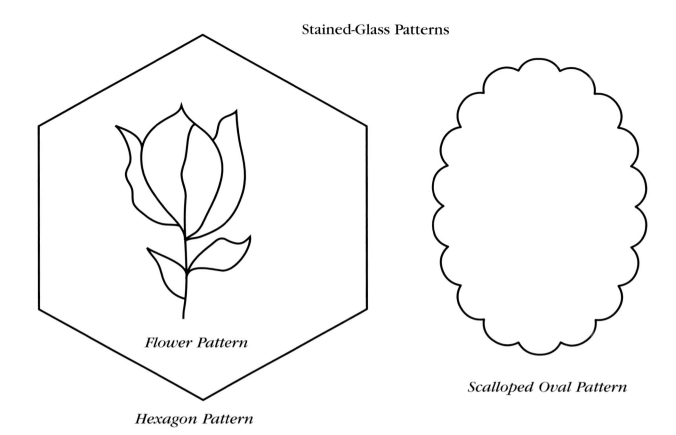

Flower Pattern

Hexagon Pattern

Scalloped Oval Pattern

Working from the outside in, flood the leaves first. Then flood the outside petals. Allow each section of the flower to dry slightly before flooding the neighboring petals. For two-toned petals, pipe half of the petal in one color and then immediately pipe another color right next to the first color. Use a toothpick to slightly blend the colors. When they are dry, pipe veins and stamens with green-colored Meringue Powder Royal Icing.

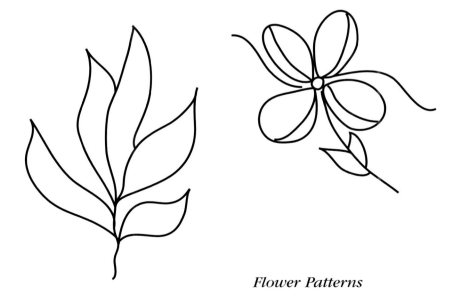

Flower Patterns

Satin-Stitch Design

These cookies provide a lovely touch when presented at a party for sewing and quilting get-togethers.

Icing: White Modeling Chocolate, Rolled Fondant, Glacé Icing, Meringue Powder Royal Icing, and Meringue Powder Flood Icing ▨ pages 133, 131, 137, 135, and 136
Suggested Cookie: Shortbread I ▨ page 128

PROCEDURE

Follow the recipe directions for making Shortbread I. Trace the pattern and place it on the rolled-out dough. Cut carefully with an X-acto knife or use cookie cutters in similar shapes. Bake and cool the cookies according to directions. When ready to ice, make five icings, White Modeling Chocolate, Rolled Fondant, Glacé Icing, Meringue Powder Royal Icing, and Meringue Powder Flood Icing.

Color the White Modeling Chocolate and Rolled Fondant in beige or ivory tones. Color some Glacé Icing in a nut-brown tone. Roll and cut the pastes. Carefully place the rolled icing on two of the cookies that have been brushed with Sieved Apricot Jam. Trim with an X-acto knife for a neat finish. Outline and flood one of the cookies with Glacé Icing.

Transfer the pattern onto the cookies. Color some Meringue Powder Royal Icing a nut-brown color. Also, color some Meringue Powder Flood Icing in nut brown.

Monogram

Outline the monogram. Flood the monogram with Meringue Powder Flood Icing for a raised look. Outline and flood the bells and leaves. Let them dry for 2 to 4 hours. With a small parchment cone with a #0 metal tip, half-fill the bag with nut-brown Meringue Powder Royal Icing.

In a zigzag motion, pipe lines back and forth over the raised surface—turning the cookie as you pipe (see Zigzag Piping). For the bell design, divide the bell straight down the middle and pipe one side of the bell in the zigzag motion, and then pipe the other side.

Pipe the stems using the same technique. For the bell design, dust the edge of the cookie with yellow petal dust. Pipe some scroll designs.

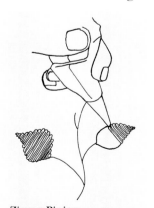

Zigzag Piping

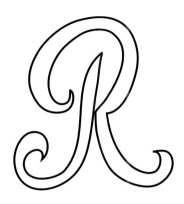

Monogram Pattern

Scalloped Round Cookie Pattern

Flower Pattern

Flower Pattern

Textile & Quilt Design

These cookies are very artsy-crafty. They have an offbeat look that can work for an offbeat affair.

Icing: Meringue Powder Royal Icing, Rolled Fondant, and Glacé Icing ▨ pages 135, 131, and 137

Suggested Cookie: Shortbread I ▨ page 128

PROCEDURE
Follow the recipe directions for making Shortbread I. Trace the pattern and place it on the rolled-out dough. Cut carefully with an X-acto knife or use cookie cutters in similar shapes. Bake and cool the cookies according to directions. When ready to ice, make three icings, Meringue Powder Royal Icing, Rolled Fondant, and Glacé Icing.

Top Cookie
Brush the cookie with Sieved Apricot Jam. Roll out the Rolled Fondant to ⅛ inch (0.3 cm) thick. Cut the Rolled Fondant with the same size cookie cutter as the cookie. Carefully place it on the glazed cookie. Neatly trim it with an X-acto knife. Stitch the perimeter of the cookie with a quilting tool. Measure and divide the cookie into fourths. Turn the cookie clockwise one-fourth turn and measure the cookie again into fourths. Score the cookie with the quilting tool in both measured directions, making a total of 16 individual sections. Pipe lines into a continuous circle on some squares; outline some sections, and flood them with different colors of Glacé Icing. Marble some, pipe dots on some, and pipe zigzag lines on others.

Middle Cookie
Trace the pattern and place it on an un-iced cookie (using the carbon-copy technique). Outline the pattern and perimeter of the cookie with Meringue Powder Royal Icing. Make up different colors of Glacé Icing. Flood the individual sections, marbling some, piping dots on some, and leaving others plain. Once dried, over-pipe each section of the cookies with Meringue Powder Royal Icing.

Bottom Cookie
Take a small portion of white Rolled Fondant and begin rolling it out. Take some lavender and blue Rolled Fondant and place pieces of it on the white fondant. Roll the fondant, achieving a tie-dyed or marbled look. Cut it with a cookie cutter and place it on an apricot-glazed cookie. Carefully trim.

Take a small blossom cutter and make floral impressions into the fondant (see Blossom Cutter). Take an even smaller blossom cutter and emboss the center of each flower. Pipe dots with Meringue Powder Royal Icing.

Over-Piping

This technique is used to create a three-dimensional effect. Outline the cookie. Let it dry for five minutes. Outline the cookie again, with the same color or a contrasting color. This technique is also used in Christmas cookie designs.

Quilt or Origami Pattern

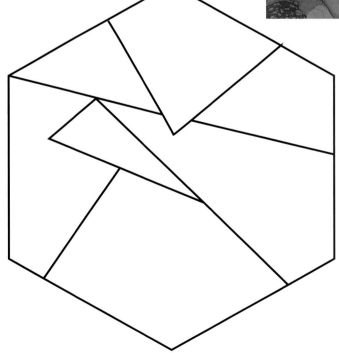

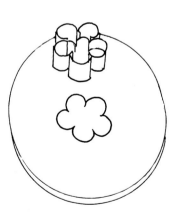

Blossom Cutter

Brush Embroidery

White brush embroidery is often seen on fine off-white linens. The edges are slightly raised and the center appears flat. Transferring this technique onto cookies is simple, but the effects are stunning.

Icing: Meringue Powder Royal Icing, Rolled Fondant, and Chocolate Rolled Fondant ▩ pages 135, 131, and 132

Suggested Cookie: Butter Cookies, Shortbread I, or Chocolate Cookies ▩ pages 124, 128, and 127

PROCEDURE

Follow the recipe directions for making Butter Cookies, Shortbread I, or Chocolate Cookies. Trace the pattern and place it on the rolled-out dough. Cut carefully with an X-acto knife or use cookie cutters in similar shapes. Bake and cool the cookies according to directions. When ready to ice, make three icings, Meringue Powder Royal Icing, White Rolled Fondant, and Chocolate Rolled Fondant.

Brush the cookies lightly with Sieved Apricot Jam. Roll out the icings to ⅛ inch (0.3 cm) thick. Cut out the icings. Carefully pick up the icing, using an offset metal spatula, and place the icing on top of the cookie, lightly pressing from the center to the edge of the cookie. If you press too hard, you will stretch the icing too much, and will then need to cut off any excess with a paring knife or an X-acto knife. Cover the rest of the

cookies. Before the rolled icing dries, use a quilting or dressmaker's wheel to outline the cookies, creating a stitching effect (see Stitching, page 105).

Carefully trace the pattern on a small piece of parchment or tracing paper. Place the pattern on the iced cookie. Using a straight pin, pinprick the pattern through the parchment onto the icing (see Transferring Design, page 105). When you remove the pattern, the pinpricked design will appear on the icing. Do this on all of the cookies.

Or you can buy many different types of cookie cutter, such as those used for gumpaste flowers (blossom and wildflower cutters), and press the cutter into the rolled icing (see Cutter).

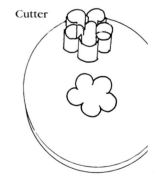

Cutter

Make the Meringue Powder Royal Icing. Color the icing with paste or gel food coloring. Be careful not to make the colors too intense.

Make up several paper cones. Half-fill each paper cone with icing. Cut a small hole in the bag, or fit the paper cone with a #2 or #3 round metal piping tip and then fill the paper cone with icing. Place the paper cones with icing under a damp sponge to prevent the icing from drying.

Starting with the farthest area from the center of the flower (usually any leaves that accompany a flower), pipe an outline around the first petal, if any. Then, with a small damp paintbrush, brush the icing from the top toward the base of the leaf (or the center of the flower when you work on petals), leaving an edge around the leaf and gradually pulling the brush toward you as you reach the base (see Painting Brush Embroidery).

As you pull the icing toward you, it is very important that you are able to see through the icing and faintly see the background rolled icing. This is the effect you want. Go to the next leaf and repeat the same procedure. After all the leaves are done, start with the flower, petal by petal, brushing the icing toward the center of the flower.

Once the flower and leaves are complete and dried, pipe veins in the leaves and stamens in the center of the flowers, then lightly brush the center of the flowers with petal dust or pearl-luster dusting colors to achieve a colorful or luminous look. For a more upscale look, pipe and gild monograms. Finish with "S"-scroll embroidery.

Marbling Technique

Roll out a piece of Dark Modeling Chocolate or Chocolate Rolled Fondant. Take pieces of white and peach-colored Rolled Fondant and stud the Dark Modeling Chocolate. Roll everything as one marbleized piece. Cut with a large round cookie cutter and carefully place it on a large cookie that has been brushed with Sieved Apricot Jam. Stitch the edge for a neater look.

Pipe "S" scrolls and embroidery around the edge of the cookie. Finish off the sides of the cookie with a ⅛-inch (0.3-cm) gold ribbon.

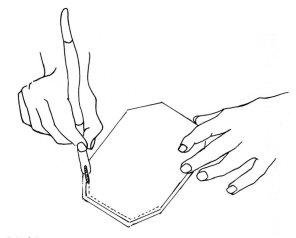

Stitching

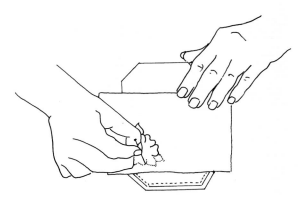

Transferring Design (using pinpricks on stencil)

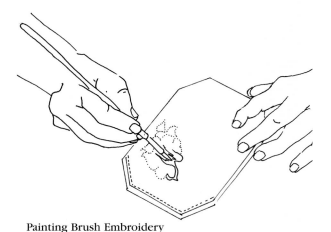

Painting Brush Embroidery

Conventional brush embroidery (left) has a somewhat flat appearance, and Victorian brush embroidery (below) has a slightly raised design.

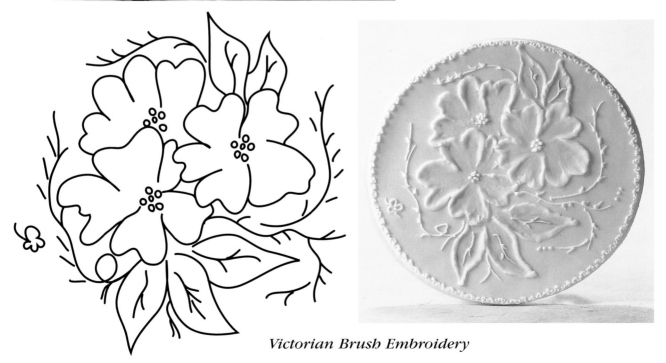

Victorian Brush Embroidery

Victorian Brush Embroidery

Victorian brush embroidery has a raised relief and flowers lightly dusted with petal dust for an elegant finish. This design creates a gift almost suitable for hanging.

Icing: Meringue Powder Royal Icing and Rolled Fondant ▪ pages 135 and 131
Suggested Cookie: Shortbread I or II ▪ pages 128 and 129

PROCEDURE

Follow the recipe directions for making Shortbread I or II. Trace the pattern and place it on the rolled-out dough. Cut carefully with an X-acto knife or use cookie cutters in similar shapes. Bake and cool the cookies according to directions. When ready to ice, make two icings, Meringue Powder Royal Icing and Rolled Fondant.

Glaze and ice the cookie with Rolled Fondant. Let the fondant dry for 2 hours. Transfer the pattern to the fondant-covered cookie. Outline each petal with a #3 or #4 round tip and Meringue Powder Royal Icing. Immediately brush the icing to the center of the flower, using a little water and leaving a transparent film of icing and a thicker edge to the petal. Outline petal by petal (see Outlining Petals) and follow through with the brush stroke (see Painting Brush Embroidery, page 105).

This outline in thicker icing will create a raised relief, characteristic of this Victorian style.

After the petals and leaves are all brushed, let them dry for 2 to 4 hours. Then pipe dots for stamens in the center of each flower and veins in the leaves with a #0 metal tip. Pipe some branches with little twigs growing off them. Pipe Cornelli lace around the perimeter of the cookie.

Finally, lightly brush petal dust inside each petal and the leaves for a soft Victorian look.

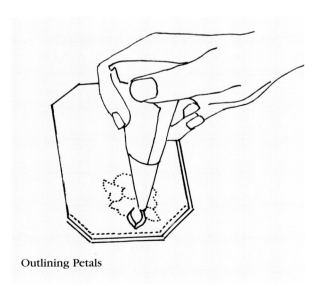

Outlining Petals

Quick & Easy Textures

These cookie-press designs and designs that use sugar crystals and sprinkles are fun and easy. The cookies are great for a picnic, a beach party, or other occasion. Kids can get into the act, too.

Cookie-Press Design

Icing: Rolled Fondant, White Modeling Chocolate, and Meringue Powder Royal Icing ▪ pages 131, 133, and 135
Suggested Cookie: Butter Cookies ▪ page 124

PROCEDURE

Follow the recipe directions for making Butter Cookies. Trace the pattern and place it on the rolled-out dough. Cut carefully with an X-acto knife or use cookie cutters in similar shapes. Bake and cool the cookies according to directions. When ready to ice, make three icings, Rolled Fondant, White Modeling Chocolate, and Meringue Powder Royal Icing.

Traditional Method

Roll out the cookie dough to ¼ inch (0.6 cm) and push the cookie press directly into the dough. Then cut out the dough with a cookie cutter and carefully place it on a baking tray to bake. After they are baked, the cookie will have a pretty impression of a design made by the cookie press.

This alone is simple and pretty enough for presentation. When they cool, you can dust the cookies with petal dust in various colors for a soft look.

Alternate Method

Roll and cut the cookie dough with various cookie cutters. When they're cool, brush the cookies with Sieved Apricot Jam. For a raised look, roll small amounts of White Modeling Chocolate into ½-inch (1.25-cm) balls. Slightly flatten them and place one in the center of each cookie. Roll the Rolled Fondant ⅛ to ¼ inch (0.3 to 0.6 cm) thick. Emboss it with the cookie press. Cut out the embossed sections with a cookie cutter that will fit over the embossed section and that's large enough to cover the entire cookie. Place cutouts over the cookies (with the white-chocolate centers). Carefully pat the edges to seal the icing to the cookie.

Petal dust the raised designs on the cookies, or slightly moisten the petal dust with lemon extract and paint the designs with a small pointed sable brush. Pipe dots or embroidery to finish the designs.

Sugar Crystals & Sprinkles

Icing: Meringue Powder Royal Icing ▪ page 135

Additions: Assorted Sprinkles and Crystallized Sugar

Suggested Cookie: Butter Cookies or Chocolate Cookies ▪ pages 124 and 127

PROCEDURE

Follow the recipe directions for making Butter Cookies or Chocolate Cookies. Trace the pattern and place it on the rolled-out dough. Cut carefully with an X-acto knife or use cookie cutters in similar shapes.

Sugar Crystals & Sprinkles

Bake and cool the cookies according to directions. When ready to ice, make the Meringue Powder Royal Icing.

Brush the cookies with Sieved Apricot Jam, corn syrup, or honey, etc. Place one of the cookies in a shallow bowl. Pour the sprinkles onto the cookie. Press lightly. Remove the cookie from the sprinkles and let the excess fall into the shallow bowl. Adorn the cookie with small Meringue Powder Royal Icing flowers or pipe dots or a bow. Gild with gold.

Cookie Press Designs

Floral Basket

This floral basket makes a lovely gift for any occasion. You could present it as a birthday, get-well, or bridal-shower gift.

Icing: Rolled Fondant and Meringue Powder Royal Icing ▪ pages 131 and 135
Suggested Cookie: Shortbread I ▪ page 128

PROCEDURE

Follow the recipe directions for making Shortbread I. Trace the pattern and place it on the rolled-out dough. Cut carefully with an X-acto knife or use cookie cutters in similar shapes. Bake and cool the cookies according to directions. When ready to ice, make two icings, Rolled Fondant and Meringue Powder Royal Icing.

Basket Weave

Measure out some Rolled Fondant. Color the paste a dark or nut brown. Dust the surface with a little cornstarch. Roll out the paste about ¼ inch (0.6 cm) thick. With a basket-weave rolling pin, roll the pin over the paste with even and medium pressure (see Basket-Weave Rolling Pin). This will imprint a basket-weave design on the paste and it will thin the paste to approximately ⅛ inch (0.3 cm) thick.

Cut it with a basket cookie cutter or place a traced pattern on the paste. Cut out the basket. Brush the cookie with Sieved Apricot Jam and carefully attach the icing to the cookie.

Basket Handle

To create the handle, take the brown paste and knead some white vegetable shortening into the paste to prevent it from sticking. Roll it into a ½-inch-thick (1.25-cm-thick) log, about 3½ inches (8.9 cm) long. Put the paste into a clay gun with the three-petal disk (see Clay Gun on page 95).

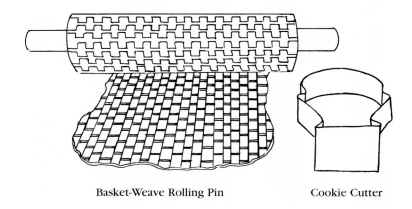

Basket-Weave Rolling Pin   **Cookie Cutter**

Put the plunger inside the gun and push on the plunger handle until the scored paste protrudes through the other end of the gun. Continue until you use up all the paste inside the gun. Gently twist the scored paste to resemble a rope. Attach the rope around the top of the basket. Cut off any excess with an X-acto knife. Attach bows to the end of each handle with a dot of Meringue Powder Royal Icing.

Finish off by piping rosettes and leaves (see drawing right).

Piping Rosettes and Leaves

Basket Pattern

Lattice Design

First, brush the cookie with Sieved Apricot Jam. Color Rolled Fondant a pale peach color. Roll out to ⅛ inch (0.3 cm) thick. Cut with a basket cutter and carefully place the fondant on the cookie. Make a medium-size parchment cone. Cut and fit it with a #2 or 3 round tip. Fill the bag half-full with white Meringue Powder Royal Icing. Score the top edge of the basket from left to right with a dressmaker's tool. This will mark the edge of the lattice design. Start at the top left or right. Pipe diagonal lines approximately ⅛ to ¼ inch (0.3 to 0.6 cm) apart. Pipe from one end to the other (see Basket with Lattice Piping).

Let the icing dry for 15 minutes. Repeat the design, starting at the opposite end and piping so that the lines crisscross. Let this dry for 15 minutes. Outline the edge of the lattice for a neater look. Finish off with rosettes and leaves and a cascading ribbon.

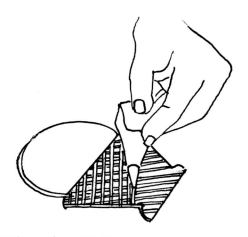

Basket with Lattice Piping

Brush-Painting & Stencil Design

This brush-painting and stencil design appeals to the hidden artist within. It combines stenciling and a loose, steady hand. Present this cookie to someone special.

Icing: Rolled Fondant and Meringue Powder Royal Icing ▪ pages 131 and 135
Additions: Paste Food Colors and Liquid Whitener
Suggested Cookie: Shortbread I ▪ page 128

PROCEDURE

Follow the recipe directions for making Shortbread I. Trace the pattern and place it on the rolled-out dough. Cut carefully with an X-acto knife or use cookie cutters in similar shapes. Bake and cool the cookies according to directions. When ready to ice, make two icings, Rolled Fondant and Meringue Powder Royal Icing.

Brush the cookie with Sieved Apricot Jam before attaching the Rolled Fondant. Allow the fondant to dry on the cookie for 2 to 4 hours. Place a similar type of stencil on the cookie and transfer the pattern with Meringue Powder Royal Icing (see page 22). Let the icing dry for 1 hour.

Practice brush strokes on cardboard before attempting to paint the finished cookie. Hold the brush at a 90° angle. Dip the brush in water and then into paste or gel food coloring mixed with liquid whitener. Move the brush in an upward motion, applying light pressure to create the base of the leaf or petal. Then, apply a heavier pressure to create a wide leaf or petal, easing up on pressure and finishing with a light stroke to form the tip of the leaf. This is the basic stroke for making a leaf or petal. Continue to practice until your strokes are fluid.

Pull out stems from the leaves with thin strokes and paint five dots for florets on the stems and around the leaves. Practice the technique until you have a natural flow and ease with the brush. When ready, paint leaves and stems, starting at the bottom of the stencil design and extending the design on up throughout the stencil. Finish the design with dots of florets in complementary colors. Let it dry for several hours.

Cookie Box

This is the ultimate cookie box. Fill it with beautifully decorated cookies, truffles, chocolate, or marzipan. We've decorated ours with brush-painted violets.

Icing: Rolled Fondant and Meringue Powder Royal Icing — pages 131 and 135
Additions: Gel Food Color and Quick Gum Paste — page 139
Suggested Cookie: Shortbread I or Shortbread II — pages 128 and 129

PROCEDURE
Follow the recipe directions for making Shortbread I or Shortbread II. Trace the pattern and place it on the rolled-out dough. Cut carefully with an X-acto knife or use cookie cutters in similar shapes. Bake and cool the cookies according to directions. When ready to ice, make two icings, Rolled Fondant and Meringue Powder Royal Icing. Also make some Quick Gum Paste.

Box Design
To complete this box, you'll need: 2 octagonal (top and bottom) and 8 square or rectangular (side panel) cookies, 1 large octagonal plaque (lid) made of Quick Gum Paste, 1 ribbon strip, and 1 bow.

Side-Panel Cookies (8)
Brush the 8 cookies with Sieved Apricot Jam. Color and roll out lavender-colored Rolled Fondant.

Place a piece of ornate lace on top of the fondant. Make sure that you lightly brush a little white vegetable shortening onto the lace to prevent it from sticking to the fondant. Apply even and firm pressure as you roll the rolling pin over the lace. Remove the lace to reveal a beautiful pattern on the Rolled Fondant.

Cut the fondant with a rectangular or square cutter, or place a pattern on the design over the fondant and cut with an X-acto knife. Place and fit each cutout over each cookie.

Top & Bottom Panel Cookies (2)
Add white Rolled Fondant to the purple or lavender fondant for a lighter shade. Roll out the fondant, but do not emboss it with lace. Cut it out and attach it to the cookies brushed with Sieved Apricot Jam. Let the icing dry for 6 to 12 hours before transferring the floral design to the top panel only.

Box Lid (1)
Color the Quick Gum Paste a deep shade of purple or lavender. Roll to ⅛ inch (0.3 cm) thick. Cut it out with a cookie cutter or pattern. Let the gum paste dry for 12 hours on one side and 12 on the opposite side.

Floral Panel

Transfer the pattern to the cookie. Mix a palette of colors: purple and pink with variations of each shade. Add a little Liquid Whitener to bring out the pastel shade of each color.

With a small flat filbert brush and a little water, dip the brush into a little color or a combination of colors and brush from the top of the petal to the center of the flower. Paint the opposite petal, allowing the petals to dry before painting petals that overlap. Change the tones of petals within one flower (see Brush-Painting Petal Tones).

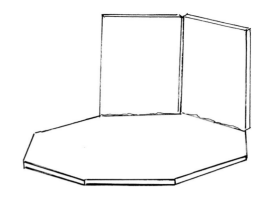

Cookie Box Construction

Brush-Painting Petal Tones

After the petals have been painted, allow them to dry for 2 to 4 hours. Paint the stamens with a fine-pointed brush in a darker shade.

With a dry brush, apply lavender or purple petal dust around the perimeter of the cookie for a softer look. Outline the edge with white Meringue Powder Royal Icing. Set aside to dry.

Assembly

Put the bottom cookie on a piece of parchment or wax paper. Attach panels (eight iced squares) with a little Meringue Powder Royal Icing at the bottom of each panel. Put an object in front of or in back of each panel to support it. Allow each panel to dry in position (see Cookie Box Construction). There will be spaces between each panel. Allow the panels to dry for 6 to 12 hours before adding the top.

Ribbon

Roll out the Rolled Fondant, tinted a deep purple, and cut a long strip for the ribbon. Apply a little water on the back of the strip. Attach it around the box's middle, starting and ending in front of the box. Cut off any excess with an X-acto knife.

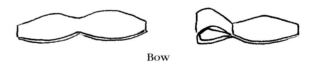

Bow

Cut a large bow freehand from Rolled Fondant (see Bow) and cut a thin strip to wrap around its middle. Secure each bow end and the middle piece with a drop of water. Let it dry for 2 to 4 hours.

Cut out rectangular strips of light and dark colors and attach them over the seams (where the panels join together). Covering the box seams isn't necessary, but it gives the illusion that this is not a box made of cookies.

Finally, apply a little Meringue Powder Royal Icing on the top of each panel. Attach the Quick-Gum-Paste lid. Apply a little icing in the middle of the lid and attach the floral-print cookie panel. cookies. Attach the bow with a little icing.

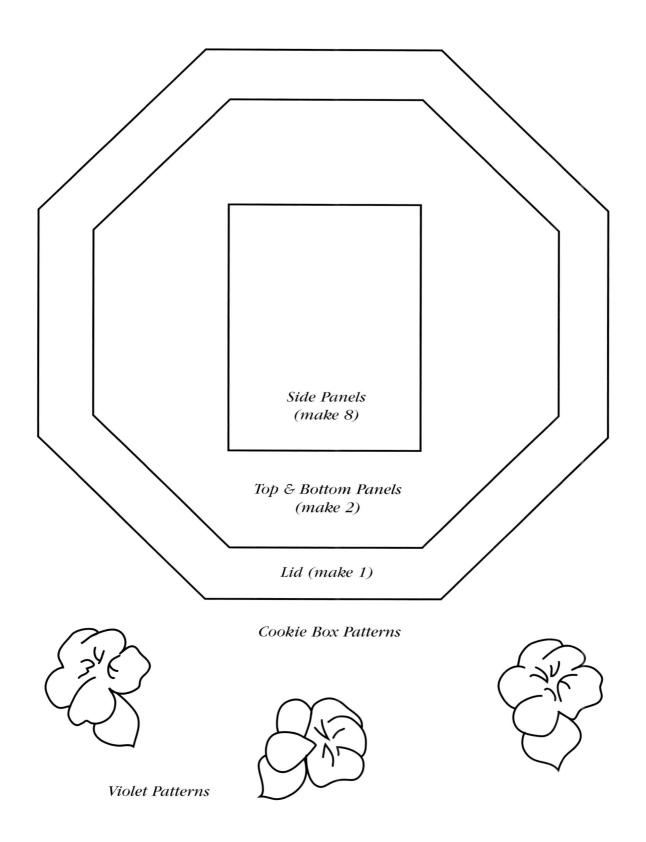

Side Panels
(make 8)

Top & Bottom Panels
(make 2)

Lid (make 1)

Cookie Box Patterns

Violet Patterns

Appliqué Design

This appliqué design is bold yet pretty, elegant but simple. Adorn a semiformal table with these tulip and five-petal floral delights.

Icing: Dark Modeling Chocolate and Rolled Fondant ▪ pages 133 and 131
Suggested Cookie: Chocolate Cookies or Butter Cookies ▪ pages 127 and 124

PROCEDURE

Follow the recipe directions for making Chocolate Cookies or Butter Cookies. Trace the pattern and place it on the rolled-out dough. Cut carefully with an X-acto knife or use cookie cutters in similar shapes. Bake and cool the cookies according to directions. When ready to ice, make two icings, Dark Modeling Chocolate and Rolled Fondant.

Cookies

Brush the cookies with Sieved Apricot Jam. Roll out the Dark Modeling Chocolate. Cut it with a cookie cutter or pattern and attach the icing to the cookies.

Tulip

Color some Rolled Fondant in a pale color (peach, pink, or yellow). Also color some Rolled Fondant in pale green. Trace and cut out the pattern for tulips. Press the tulip cutout against a sil-

icone tulip mold or the back of a washed and dried real tulip petal. Lightly soften the edges of the cutouts with a dog-bone or ball tool. Be careful not to ruffle the petal.

Roll out peach and green Rolled Fondant and cut out leaves in each color (see Leaf Patterns) by hand. Use petal dust on the petals in an accompanying color. Overlap and attach the tulip petals with a little moisture (water). Attach green leaves on top and peach leaves on top of green leaves. Finish off the bottom of the flower with a five-petal cut-out blossom. Attach with water. Score the center of the flower with a rounded toothpick.

Five-Petal Flower

Cut five petals in a pale pink Rolled Fondant. Cut out three petals in Dark Modeling Chocolate. Cut out two petals in pale green Rolled Fondant and cut out a five-petal blossom. Emboss leaves with a silicone leaf press or use the back of a real rose leaf and soften edges (see pages 50–51). Use petal dust on the pink petals in darker shades of the pink. Also use petal dust on the pale green leaves.

Attach the five pink petals first; make sure that all points meet in the center. Secure them with a little water. Attach the green leaves at 9 o'clock and 3 o'clock, slightly under the petals at each position. Attach the chocolate petals evenly with points meeting in the center. Place the blossom cutout on top. Pipe the stamens with leftover white Meringue Powder Royal Icing.

Leaf and Petal Patterns

Leaf and Petal Patterns

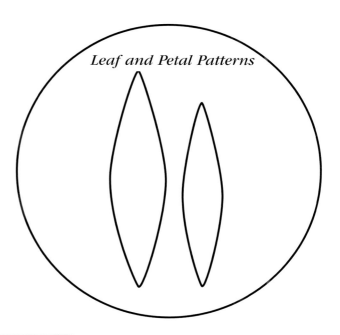

Round Cookie Pattern

Tulip Petal Pattern

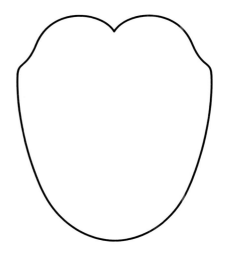

Fan Design

This frilly and feminine cookie will please an adoring grand-mother, art lover, needlecraft hobbyist, or someone who loves elegant details.

Icing: Glacé Icing, Meringue Powder Royal Icing, and Rolled Fondant ▬ pages 137, 135, and 131
Additions: Gilding ▬ page 138
Suggested Cookie: Butter Cookies or Shortbread I ▬ pages 124 and 128

PROCEDURE
Follow the recipe directions for making Butter Cookies or Shortbread I. Trace the pattern and place it on the rolled-out dough. Cut carefully with an X-acto knife or use cookie cutters in similar shapes. Bake and cool the cookies according to directions. When ready to ice, make three icings, Glacé Icing, Meringue Powder Royal Icing, and Rolled Fondant.

Fan
Outline the fan-shaped cookie in Meringue Powder Royal Icing. Make a batch of Glacé Icing. Color the icing in two different tones, white and ivory or any other two-color combinations, e.g., pink and white, peach and white, purple and lavender, etc.

Flood the first panel in a dark shade. Skip over the second panel for now. Flood the third panel in a dark shade. Allow the icing to crust over for 2 hours. After 2 hours, flood the second panel in a lighter shade and flood the fourth panel in a lighter shade. Let this dry for 2 hours.

Fan Handle
Flood the handle in a light tone. Let it dry for 2 hours. Pipe Cornelli lace around the edge of the handle. Dry for 20 minutes; then gild with gold.

Buttons
Roll out different shades of Rolled Fondant (white, lavender, purple, ivory, etc). Take the wide end of a #4 round metal piping tip and press and cut out a button. Use the end of a thin paintbrush and push through the hole in the #4 tip to push out the button shape. Use a #1 or #2 round tip to score two buttonholes. Repeat this procedure until you have buttons in different shades.

Rope
Take a piece of Rolled Fondant in different shades of white, ivory, and brown. Slightly knead them together while maintaining a marbled look. Take a piece of the marbled fondant and roll it into a thin sausage. Place the sausage

into the barrel of a clay gun fitted with a three-petal disk. Press the plunger to release the scored paste. Continue to press until you have a piece of paste that's 5 to 6 inches (12.5 to 15 cm) long. Cut off the excess. Use both hands to twist the paste in opposite directions to create a rope. Pinch one end to seal the rope (see photo right).

Tassel

Change the disk in the clay gun to a multi-hole disk. If you used up the paste to make the rope, put additional paste in the clay gun. Press on the plunger to reveal spaghettilike strings (see Clay Gun and Disk). Continue to press until you have strings about 2 inches (5 cm) long. Gather the strings at the end of the barrel and tear them off with your fingers. Be careful when handling them because they are very delicate. Lay this bunch aside. Make another bunch of strings and tear them off at the barrel.

Lay both bunches together and pinch them off to hold them together. Then pinch both string bunches to the other end of the rope, being careful not to misshape the rope. Slightly frill and separate the strings. Let them dry (see tassel in photo).

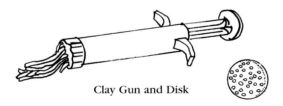

Clay Gun and Disk

Assembly

Put some Meringue Powder Royal Icing in a small parchment cone fitted with a #0 metal tip. Pipe embroidery around the left and right shoulders of the fan. Use the same tip to pipe Swiss dots sporadically on the fan. Use a #2 or 3 round metal tip with Meringue Powder Royal Icing to create an edge with over-piping between the second and third panels. Attach the buttons with tiny dots of Meringue Powder Royal Icing. Place the tassel with rope under the fan.

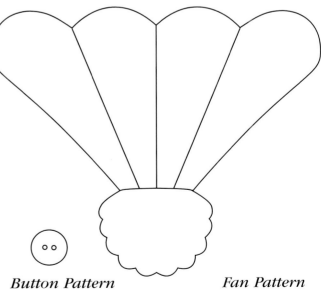

Button Pattern   *Fan Pattern*

Photocopy patterns at 200%.

"China" Plate

This makes a lovely centerpiece for a festive family gathering. The plate can be enlarged and filled with wrapped candies, miniature marzipan fruits, or petit fours.

Icing: Rolled Fondant and Meringue Powder Royal Icing ▨ pages 131 and 135
Additions: Paste Food Colors and Liquid Whitener
Suggested Cookie: Shortbread II ▨ page 129

PROCEDURE

Follow the recipe directions for making Shortbread II. Trace the pattern and place it on the rolled-out dough. Cut carefully with an X-acto knife or use cookie cutters in similar shapes. Bake and cool the cookies according to directions. When ready to ice, make two icings, Rolled Fondant and Meringue Powder Royal Icing.

As soon as the cookie comes out of the oven, prepare a saucer that's lightly dusted with all-purpose flour. Let the cookie cool for five minutes on the baking tray. Carefully remove the large round cookie with a wide spatula. Place it on the saucer and carefully press it onto the plate. Let the cookie dry overnight.

The next day, remove the cookie from the saucer and place it on parchment paper backside up. Let it dry for 12 hours. After it has dried, brush the plate with Sieved Apricot Jam and ice with Rolled Fondant.

Painting & Design

Put a plain round cookie cutter on the iced china-plate-shaped cookie that's smaller than the "china plate." With a quilting tool, score the cookie around the inside of the cookie cutter. Place another plain round cookie cutter on the cookie that's larger than the previous cutter. With a quilting tool, score inside it on the cookie. Use these concentric-circle guidelines as sections for the plate.

Mix paste or gel food color with liquid whitener to achieve a pastel shade. Use a medium-size paintbrush to paint the inside circle with a light color; be careful not to go over the quilted line. Let it dry for 1 hour.

Paint the next circle with a darker color that's mixed with liquid whitener. Carefully paint the cookie, making sure that you don't go over the quilted line. Let the icing dry for 2 to 4 hours. Pipe fine "S"-scroll embroidery within the dark shade. Gild the scrolls.

Gild the edge of the plate. Let it dry for 1 hour. Cut out a pear shape with a small cookie cutter. Place the pear cutout on the center of the plate. Dust the cutout with petal dust to achieve a more natural tone. (See the finished china-plate cookie in the photo on page 123, opposite.)

Recipes

You'll enjoy making these recipes for delicious cookies; glacé, meringue, and rolled icings; modeling chocolates; rolled fondants; gum paste; gilding; and much more. We've also revealed professional hints from cookie and cake masters.

Butter Cookies

Yield: up to 3½ dozen cookies

This is my favorite cookie dough. It's easy, rolls out beautifully, and tastes great.

INGREDIENTS

1 cup (8 oz or 230 g) unsalted butter

1 cup (8 oz or 230 g) granulated sugar

1 large egg

1 tsp baking powder

1 tsp pure vanilla extract

3 cups (12 oz or 340 g) all-purpose flour, plus extra for rolling out dough

Preheat oven to 350°F. In a large bowl, cream the butter and sugar with a mixer paddle attachment for 2 minutes. Stop and scrape the bowl. Cream the mixture for an additional 60 seconds. Beat in the egg and vanilla extract. Beat until well combined.

Sift together baking powder and flour. Add the flour mixture 1 cup (4 oz or 112 g) at a time to the creamed butter and sugar mixture. Mix thoroughly after each addition. Blend in the last cup of flour by hand. The dough will be stiff.

Divide the dough into two balls. Wrap one ball into plastic wrap until ready to use. On a floured surface, roll out the other ball ⅛ inch (0.3 cm) thick. Use a large offset metal spatula to run under the dough to prevent it from sticking. Cut out cookies with cookie cutters, dipping the cutters into flour before each use.

Carefully place the cut-out cookies onto an ungreased nonstick cookie sheet or a parchment-lined half-sheet pan. Bake for 6 to 8 minutes or until the edges of the cookies begin to brown lightly. Let the cookies rest on the cookie sheet until ready to use.

Note: This dough can be rolled out immediately after making. Also, this dough can be made in advance. Wrap the dough well in plastic wrap and then place it in a zippered plastic bag. The dough will last at least 2 weeks in the refrigerator and up to 2 months if frozen. For a denser cookie, omit the baking powder.

Lemon & Orange Cream Cookies

Yield: up to 4 dozen cookies

This orange or lemon variation is softer than the Butter Cookies recipe because of the addition of heavy cream. This dough can be rolled right after preparation; however, use lighter pressure. If wrapped and refrigerated for 1 hour before rolling, the dough will roll out more easily.

INGREDIENTS

1 cup (8 oz or 230 g) unsalted butter

1 cup (8 oz or 230 g) granulated sugar

1 large egg

1 tsp baking powder

1 tsp lemon extract OR orange extract

2 Tbsp heavy cream

zest of large lemon OR medium orange

3½ cups (14 oz or 392 g) all-purpose flour, plus extra for rolling out dough

Preheat oven to 350°F. Cream the butter and sugar for 2 minutes. Stop and scrape the bowl. Cream the mixture for an additional 60 seconds. Add the egg, lemon or orange extract, heavy cream, and zest of lemon or orange (depending on the extract you choose) to the creamed butter and sugar mixture. Beat until well combined. Follow the rest of the procedure for making Butter Cookies.

Note: This dough can be refrigerated for 3 to 5 days or frozen for at least 2 weeks.

Almond Paste Cookies

I like this cookie, because it doesn't have an overwhelming almond taste. For a chewier cookie, add up to 1 oz (28 g) of additional almond paste.

INGREDIENTS

¾ cup (6 oz or 168 g) unsalted butter

4 oz (112 g) almond paste

1 cup (8 oz or 230 g) granulated sugar

1 large egg

1 egg yolk

1 tsp almond extract

2½ cups (10 oz or 280 g) all-purpose flour, plus extra for rolling out dough

1 tsp baking powder

½ tsp salt

Preheat oven to 350°F. In a large bowl, cream the butter, sugar, and almond paste with a mixer's paddle attachment for 2 minutes. Stop and scrape the bowl. Cream the mixture for an additional 60 seconds. Beat in the whole egg, the yolk, and the almond extract. Beat until the liquid is well combined and absorbed.

Sift together the baking powder, salt, and flour. Add flour mixture 1 cup (4 oz or 112 g) at a time to the creamed butter and sugar mixture. Mix thoroughly after each addition. Blend in the last cup of flour by hand. The dough will be stiff.

Divide the dough into two balls. Wrap one ball into plastic wrap until ready to use. On a floured surface, roll out the other ball ⅛ inch (0.3 cm) thick. Use a large offset metal spatula to run under the dough to prevent it from sticking. Use cookie cutters dipped into flour before each use to cut out the cookies.

Carefully place the cookie cutouts onto an ungreased parchment sheet or nonstick half-sheet pan. Bake for 6 to 8 minutes or until the edges of the cookies begin to brown lightly. Let the cookies rest on a cookie sheet until ready to use.

Note: This dough can be rolled out right away. It also refrigerates well; you can keep it at least 2 weeks and it can be frozen for up to 2 months.

Chocolate Cookies

This is one of my favorite cookies. It has a light chocolate taste and goes well with any type of icing.

INGREDIENTS

1 cup (8 oz or 230 g) unsalted butter

⅔ cup (5.3 oz or 150 g) granulated sugar

⅓ cup (2.6 or 75 g) dark brown sugar, packed

1 large egg

1 Tbsp extra-strong coffee OR 1 Tbsp chocolate liqueur

⅓ cup (1.2 oz or 35 g) cocoa powder, Dutch-processed

3 cups (12 oz or 336 g) all-purpose flour, plus extra for rolling out dough

½ tsp baking soda

¼ tsp salt

Preheat oven to 350°F. Cream together the butter, granulated sugar, and packed brown sugar for 2 minutes. Stop and scrape the bowl. Cream the mixture for an additional 30 to 60 seconds. Beat in the egg and coffee or chocolate liqueur. Beat until the liquid is absorbed and well combined.

Sift together the flour, cocoa powder, baking soda, and salt. Add the flour mixture 1 cup (4 oz or 112 g) at a time to the creamed mixture. Beat. Add the last cup of flour by hand.

This is a stiff dough. Divide the dough into two balls. Wrap one ball into plastic wrap until ready to use. When ready to roll, sprinkle flour onto the countertop and roll out the cookie dough to ⅛ inch (0.3 cm) thick. Run a large metal offset spatula under the dough to prevent it from sticking. Cut out the dough with a cookie cutter or traced pattern. Place the cookies on a nonstick cookie sheet or a parchment-lined sheet.

Bake for 6 to 8 minutes or until the edges of the cookies start to brown. Let the cookies cool on the cookie sheet.

Note: This dough can be made up to a few days in advance. It will last at least 2 weeks in the refrigerator and up to 2 months in the freezer.

Shortbread I

Yield: up to 3 dozen cookies

Basically, this is the Butter Cookie recipe without the baking powder and egg. The idea here is to create a dense cookie that's suitable for larger-scale decorating.

INGREDIENTS

1 cup (8 oz or 230 g) unsalted butter

1 cup (8 oz or 230 g) granulated sugar

1½ tsp pure vanilla extract

2½ cups (10 oz or 280 g) sifted all-purpose flour, plus extra for rolling out dough

Preheat oven to 350°F. Cream together the butter and sugar. Beat for 2 minutes. Stop and scrape the bowl. Cream the mixture for an additional 60 seconds. Add the vanilla. Beat until well combined.

Add the flour 1 cup (4 oz or 112 g) at a time. Add the last ½ cup (2 oz or 60 g) of flour by hand. If the dough is crumbly, wrap it in plastic wrap and refrigerate for 1 hour before rolling.

Sprinkle flour on the work surface. Roll, cut, and place the cutouts on an ungreased parchment sheet or nonstick pan, or roll the dough onto parchment or wax paper. Cut out the cookies with a cookie cutter or an X-acto knife, and remove excess dough from around the cutouts.

Lift the parchment or wax paper with the cookie cutouts and place it on a baking sheet. The paper protects a large-size cookie from breaking if you try to pick it up and place it on the baking sheet. Bake for 6 to 10 minutes, depending on the size of the cookies, or until the edges start to brown. Remove the cookies from the oven and let them cool on the baking sheet.

Note: Don't overwork the dough. Overworking the dough will produce a tough cookie. This dough can be refrigerated for up to 3 weeks and frozen for up to 2½ months.

Shortbread II

Yield: up to 3 dozen cookies

This is an alternative to Shortbread I.

INGREDIENTS

1 cup (8 oz or 230 g) unsalted butter

1 cup (8 oz or 230 g) granulated sugar

1½ tsp pure vanilla extract

⅓ cup (1.3 oz or 40 g) cornstarch

2¼ cups (9 oz or 252 g) all-purpose flour, plus extra for rolling out dough

Preheat oven to 350°F. Cream together the butter and sugar for 2 minutes. Stop and scrape the bowl. Cream the mixture for an additional 60 seconds. Add the vanilla. Beat until blended.

In a separate bowl, sift together the flour and cornstarch. Add the flour mixture 1 cup (4 oz or 112 g) at a time. Add last ½ cup (2 oz or 60 g) of flour by hand.

Sprinkle flour on the work surface. Roll, cut, and place cutouts on an ungreased parchment sheet or nonstick pan, or roll the dough onto parchment or wax paper. Cut out the cookies with a cookie cutter or an X-acto knife and remove excess from around the cutouts.

Lift the parchment or wax paper with the cutouts and place the cookies on the baking sheet. This helps protects a large-size cookie from breaking if you try to pick it up and place it on the baking sheet. Bake the cookies for 6 to 10 minutes, depending their size, or until the edges start to brown. Remove the cookies and let them cool on the baking sheet.

Note: This cookie dough will freeze for up to 3 months and can be refrigerated for up to 3 weeks.

Gingerbread Cookies

Yield: up to 5 dozen cookies

This recipe makes delicious gingerbread cookies. It's great for making a large quantity of cookies.

INGREDIENTS

1¼ cups (10 oz or 280 g) unsalted butter

⅔ cup (5.3 oz or 150 g) granulated sugar

⅓ cup (2.6 oz or 75 g) packed brown sugar

1 tsp pure vanilla extract

2 tsp ginger

1 tsp cinnamon

1 tsp nutmeg

½ cup (120 ml) whole milk

1 cup (12 oz or 336 g) unsulfured molasses

1 tsp baking soda

½ tsp salt

5½ to 6 cups (22 to 24 oz or 616 to 672 g) all-purpose flour, plus extra for rolling out dough

Preheat oven to 350°F. Cream together the butter and sugars for 3 minutes. Stop and scrape the bowl. Cream the mixture for an additional 30 seconds. Add the vanilla, ginger, cinnamon, nutmeg, milk, and molasses. Mix for an additional 2 minutes. The mixture will look speckled and broken.

Sift together the baking soda, salt, and flour. Add the flour mixture to the creamed mixture 1 cup (4 oz or 112 g) at a time. Mix the last 1½ cups (6 oz or 168 g) of flour by hand, as needed. If the dough is still sticky, add a little extra flour. Divide the dough in thirds. Wrap each in plastic wrap and refrigerate for 1 hour before rolling it out.

Sprinkle extra flour onto the counter. Roll, cut, and place the cutouts on an ungreased parchment sheet or nonstick pan. Bake the cookies for 6 to 9 minutes, depending on their size, or until the edges start to brown. Remove and let the cookies cool on the baking sheet.

Note: This dough can be refrigerated for up to 1 week and may be frozen for up to 1 month. It can be rolled out after it's made; however, because of the moisture content, it may be difficult to work with. The dough performs better if refrigerated for 1 to 2 hours before you roll it out.

Rolled Fondant

Yield: up to 2 lb (900 g) or enough to cover 2½ to 3 dozen cookies

This is a flexible sugar dough that's usually rolled out and fitted over cakes. By making this from scratch, you can control all the ingredients and get a better-tasting fondant.

INGREDIENTS

1 Tbsp (1 envelope) unflavored gelatin

¼ cup (60 ml) cold water

1 tsp lemon extract, almond extract, OR orange extract

½ cup (6 oz or 168 g) light corn syrup

1 Tbsp glycerin (optional)

up to 2 lb (900 g) 10X confectioners' sugar

½ tsp white vegetable shortening

Sprinkle the gelatin over the cold water in a small bowl. Let it stand for 2 minutes to soften. Place it over a pan of simmering water until the gelatin dissolves, or use the microwave for 30 seconds on HIGH. Do not overheat. Add flavoring.

Add the corn syrup and glycerin and stir until the mixture is smooth and clear. Gently reheat if necessary, or microwave for an additional 15 to 20 seconds on high. Stir again.

Sift 1½ pounds (680 g) of confectioners' sugar into a large bowl. Make a well in the sugar and pour in the liquid mixture. Stir with a rubber spatula. The mixture will become sticky.

Sift some of the remaining ½ pound (225 g) of sugar onto a smooth work surface and add as much of the remaining sugar as the mixture will take. Knead the fondant, adding more confectioners' sugar, if necessary, to form a smooth, pliable mass. The fondant should be firm but soft. Rub the vegetable shortening into your palms and knead it into the fondant. This relieves the stickiness of the fondant.

Wrap the fondant tightly in plastic wrap and place it in the refrigerator until ready to use. Rolled Fondant works best if allowed to rest for 24 hours.

Note: This Rolled Fondant dough can be refrigerated for several weeks if covered well. It can be frozen for up to 3 months. I do, however, recommend Pettinice RTR Icing (commercial rolled fondant). It doesn't taste quite as good as homemade; however, it has more stretch. Since it's extremely flexible, you can do more with it. This product can last for up to 6 months without refrigeration.

Chocolate Rolled Fondant

Yield: 8 oz (½ lb or 224 g) icing

This rolled icing is an alternative to Dark Modeling Chocolate.

INGREDIENTS

8 oz (224 g) Pettinice RTR Icing OR homemade Rolled Fondant (recipe on page 131)

2 to 5 Tbsp (0.2 to 0.6 oz or 6 to 16 g) cocoa powder

¼ to ½ tsp white vegetable shortening

Knead the fondant. Make a well in the center of the fondant. Add 0.2 ounce (6 g) of the cocoa powder. Knead thoroughly. Add more, a little at a time until the paste begins to thicken and becomes slightly dry. Stop adding cocoa powder and knead thoroughly. Rub the white vegetable shortening into your palms and knead into the fondant. Knead until the fondant is pliable.

Wrap it in plastic wrap and refrigerate until ready to use. This will last for weeks in the refrigerator.

Modeling Chocolates

Dark Modeling Chocolate Yield: 22 oz (616 g)

White & Milk Modeling Chocolate Yield: 20 oz (560 g)

These recipes make great-tasting chocolate rolled icings.

DARK MODELING CHOCOLATE
INGREDIENTS

1 lb (454 g) semisweet OR bittersweet dark chocolate

⅔ cup (8 oz or 224 g) light corn syrup

WHITE & MILK MODELING
CHOCOLATE INGREDIENTS

1 lb (454 g) white OR milk chocolate

½ cup (6 oz or 168 g) light corn syrup

Cut up the chocolate finely and place it in a stainless-steel bowl over a pot of boiling water. Turn off the heat under the boiling water. Let the chocolate melt, stirring occasionally until chocolate is two-thirds melted.

Remove it from the pot and stir it with a rubber spatula until it is completely melted. Pour in the corn syrup all at once and stir until the chocolate thickens and begins to leave the sides of the bowl.

Pour the chocolate into plastic wrap. Place another sheet of plastic wrap over the chocolate and flatten it out. Refrigerate for 24 hours to age. Once aged, take it out of the refrigerator and let sit for ½ hour. Cut the modeling chocolate into pieces and knead it with your palms. If the chocolate is too hard to knead, wrap it in a piece of plastic wrap and microwave for 5 to 10 seconds on HIGH. Re-knead until the chocolate is pliable. Wrap pliable pieces in zippered plastic bags. Once all the chocolate is pliable, re-knead it until the chocolate turns a beautiful shiny color. Roll, cut, and cover the cookies or make chocolate roses.

Note: Because of the fat content in the white and milk chocolates, don't over-stir the chocolate when you add in the corn syrup. Stir white or milk chocolate briefly, then pour the chocolate onto newsprint* and flatten it out. Let it rest for 2 to 4 hours to absorb some of the fat. Scrape the chocolate from the paper and lightly knead. Wrap it tightly in plastic wrap and refrigerate for 24 hours.

This rolled icing can be refrigerated for many weeks. If wrapped well and placed in an airtight container, it can keep for several months in the refrigerator.

This is a common recipe for modeling chocolate, aka "chocolate plastic" or "chocolate plastique." Many similar variations appear in decorating books and cookbooks.

* Newsprint is an inexpensive paper that happens to absorb fat. You'll find it at art-supply stores.

Egg White Royal Icing

Yield: 2½ cups (600 ml)

This decorative icing is great for outlining. This icing, preferred in cookie decorating, is perfect for embroidery and monogram piping. We recommend using pasteurized egg whites since it's uncooked.

INGREDIENTS

3 oz (84 g) fresh egg whites OR pasteurized egg whites, room-temperature

1 lb (454 g) 10X confectioners' sugar, sifted

½ tsp lemon juice

Lightly whip the egg whites on medium speed, using a paddle until the whites form soft peaks—about 3 minutes. Lower the speed and gradually add the sugar 1 cup (4 oz or 112 g) at a time. Add lemon juice and beat on medium-high speed for 5 to 8 minutes, or until the icing forms medium to stiff peaks. Cover the icing with plastic wrap until it's ready to use.

Note: This icing should be used within 1 day. For individuals sensitive to egg whites or to avoid possible salmonella food poisoning, use only pasteurized egg whites, or use the recipe for Meringue Powder Royal Icing instead.

Meringue Powder Royal Icing

Yield: 5 cups (1.2 L)

This icing avoids use of fresh (uncooked) egg whites, but it's just as versatile as Egg White Royal Icing.

INGREDIENTS

¼ cup (1.6 oz or 45 g) meringue powder

½ cup (240 ml) cold water

1 lb (454 g) 10X confectioners' sugar, sifted

½ tsp lemon juice

Add the meringue powder to the cold water in a mixing bowl. Beat to a soft-peak stage—about 3 minutes. Add the confectioners' sugar 1 cup (4 oz or 112 g) at a time. Beat between each cup. Add the lemon juice. Beat for an additional 3 to 5 minutes on medium-high speed or until the icing forms medium to stiff peaks.

Cover with plastic wrap until ready to use.

Note: This icing can be used for several weeks without refrigeration. Put the leftover icing in a brand-new plastic container with a lid or in a grease-free glass container.

Meringue Powder Flood Icing

Yield: 1 cup (240 ml)

This is the soft icing used to iced cookies. It's not too difficult to make, flows well, and dries quickly. The icing will have a flat look when diluted with water. With a little light corn syrup or pasteurized egg whites, you can get a shinier look.

INGREDIENTS

1 cup (240 ml) Meringue Powder Royal Icing

⅛ to ¼ cup (1 to 2 fl oz or 30 to 60 ml) water OR 1 to 2 oz (28 to 54 g) pasteurized egg whites

Carefully stir the water into the Meringue Powder Royal Icing a little at a time. After adding half the water, check to see if you have the right consistency. Continue to add water until you achieve a flow consistency. Add more liquid if necessary.

HOW TO CHECK FOR FLOW CONSISTENCY

You have achieved a "flow consistency" if, after you draw a knife through the icing, the icing completely comes together after you count to 10 seconds. If the icing comes together before 7 seconds, add a little more Meringue Powder Royal Icing to thicken it. Check for consistency again. If the icing doesn't come together within 10 seconds, add a little more water.

Note: This icing should be used within 3 to 5 days. Place it in a glass container and cover it with plastic wrap directly on the icing. Place a tight-fitting lid over the container. If refrigerated, this icing can last up to 1 week.

Glacé Icing

Yield: 2 cups (480 ml)

This is the chief icing used in this book. It's delicious, ridiculously easy to make, and dries to a perfect sheen. The drawback is that the icing takes a much longer time to dry. However, it's well worth the wait.

INGREDIENTS

1 lb (454 g) 10X confectioners' sugar

⅜ cup (90 ml) milk

⅜ cup (4.5 oz or 126 g) light corn syrup

Flavor Options: *1 tsp concentrated extract, 1 Tbsp alcohol or liqueur,* OR *2 to 3 drops concentrated candy oil*

In a mixing bowl, thoroughly mix the sugar and the milk first. The icing should be very soft and have a heavy-cream texture before you add the corn syrup. Add the corn syrup and mix just until combined.

Divide the icing into several bowls. Flavor each bowl with extracts, alcohol, or candy oils. Color each bowl of icing as desired. Cover the bowl with plastic wrap to prevent drying until you're ready to use it.

Note: This icing will last for up to 2 weeks in the refrigerator. Put the icing in a brand-new plastic container. Put plastic wrap directly over the icing and seal it with a tight-fitting lid. When ready to reuse, stir the icing until the icing has a flow consistency.

If you are dairy sensitive, you can replace the milk with water. Without milk, the icing can last over 3 weeks in the refrigerator.

Glacé Outline Icing

Yield: ⅔ cup (160 ml)

This icing produces a translucent outline. It gives a borderless appearance, as though the cookies were not outlined.

INGREDIENTS

½ cup (120 ml) Glacé Icing

6 to 8 heaping Tbsp (1.3 to 2 oz or 37 to 56 g) 10X confectioners' sugar

Mix until combined. The icing should be very stiff. If it's not stiff enough, add additional confectioners' sugar until you have a medium-stiff consistency. Wrap the icing with plastic wrap to prevent drying.

Note: This icing should be placed in a brand-new plastic container with plastic wrap directly over the icing and sealed with a tight-fitting lid. Refrigerate for up to 2 weeks. Re-beat the icing when you're ready to use it.

Gilding

Yield: ¼ to ½ tsp (1-2.5 ml)

Gilding can dress up the simplest design in a most elegant way.

INGREDIENTS

½ tsp powdered "gold"

2 to 6 drops lemon extract

Mix ½ teaspoon of powdered gold with a few drops of lemon extract. Stir with a small brush until you have a liquid solution. Use a sable paintbrush to brush on icing or cameos. When the alcohol evaporates, the gold turns into a solid. Add a few more drops of extract to convert it back into a liquid state. Unlike gold powder, *gold leaf* is actually 95.6% gold. This expensive decoration is quite edible.

Quick Gum Paste

Yield: 8 oz (224 g)

Gum paste is used to make beautiful lifelike flowers and small modeling projects.

INGREDIENTS

8 oz (224 g) Pettinice RTR Icing OR homemade Rolled Fondant (recipe on page 131)

1 tsp Tylose OR Tylose C

½ tsp white vegetable shortening

1 to 2 Tbsp cornstarch (to prevent sticking)

Knead fondant lightly. If sticky, knead in a little cornstarch to prevent stickiness. Shape the Rolled Fondant (or Pettinice RTR Icing) into a disk. Make a well in the Rolled Fondant. Measure the Tylose and put it in the well. Begin kneading the fondant and Tylose together. Knead for a full 3 minutes.

Rub the vegetable shortening into your palms and knead it into the gum paste. Wrap the gum paste in plastic wrap and store it in a zippered plastic bag inside an airtight container in the refrigerator. When ready to use, cut off a piece and knead it until it's pliable.

Note: Tylose C is used as a binder and thickener for Rolled Fondant. It also serves as a stabilizer in ice cream, deli, dairy, and soft-drink products.

Sieved Apricot Jam

Yield: 8 to 10 oz (224 to 280 g)

This makes a delicious coating to spread onto a cookie before it is to be covered with a rolled icing.

INGREDIENTS

8 oz (224 g) apricot preserves

½ cup (120 ml) water

Cook the preserves and water together until they begin to simmer. Strain and allow the mixture to cool. Place it in a jar with a tight-fitting lid or use an airtight container. Refrigerate until ready to use.

Note: If refrigerated, this will last for several months. This recipe will work with any other kind of fruit preserve. Although we use preserves in the recipe, the water-added and sieved result is more properly called a kind of jam, hence our recipe title Sieved Apricot Jam.

Measurements

To achieve precise measurements and best results, professional pastry chefs weigh ingredients. Ingredient measurements can be critical to the success of baked goods and other foods. If you're cooking one-pot meals, such as soups, fondues, or stews, you need not be as exacting.

Before you weigh the ingredient, first weigh the container you'll be using. Then turn your kitchen scale to "0" (zero), add the ingredient, and weigh again. Or, keeping your scale on true "0" (zero), simply deduct the weight of the container from that of the ingredient weighed in the container. For the most precise reading, use the gram weight. Remember:

1 ounce = 28 grams

1 pound = 16 ounces = 454 grams

FLOUR

When measuring flour in cookie recipes, aerate the flour, folding it about ten times, with a wire whisk in a large bowl. Then dip the measuring cup into the flour. Use an offset metal spatula to level off the flour. When sieving or sifting the flour with baking powder or baking soda and salt, add the flour first to the bowl. Then add the rising agent and salt, if required. Whisk dry ingredients briefly and then sieve or sift.

1 cup or 240 ml (8 fl oz) = 4 oz or 126 g

FLOUR

4 cups or 960 ml (16 fl oz) = 1 lb or 454 g

FLOUR

BUTTER

When using butter in recipes, measure it by weight.

1 cup or 2 sticks = 8 oz or 230 g

BUTTER

1/2 cup or 1 stick = 4 oz or 115 g

BUTTER

GRANULATED SUGAR

Measure this sugar by weight or with a dry measuring cup. Level off the sugar in the cup with a metal offset spatula.

1 cup or 240 ml = 8 oz or 230 g

GRANULATED SUGAR

2 cups or 480 ml = 16 oz or 1 lb or 455 g

GRANULATED SUGAR

10X CONFECTIONERS' SUGAR

This is finely ground granulated sugar, which we commonly call confectioners' sugar or powdered sugar. The weight of 1 cup 10X confectioners' sugar is half the weight of 1 cup granulated sugar. It's best to use 10X rather than less finely ground (XXX or XXXX) confectioners' sugars.

1 cup or 240 ml = 4 oz or 115 g

CONFECTIONERS' SUGAR

4 cups or 480 ml = 16 oz or 1 lb or 455 g

CONFECTIONERS' SUGAR

OTHER DRY INGREDIENTS

Baking powder, baking soda, salt, and spices can be measured using a measuring spoon. Level off the dry ingredient in the spoon with a knife.

1 tsp = 5 ml   1 Tbsp = 15 ml

EGGS

All recipes in this book call for large eggs. A large American-size egg with shell weighs about 2 oz or 60 g. Without the shell, it weighs about 1¾ oz or 50 g.

LIQUIDS

Water, milk, and alcohol can be measured using a liquid measuring cup. You can measure large amounts of liqueur in a liquid measuring cup, too.

1 cup = 8 FLUID oz = 240 ml

WATER, MILK, OR ALCOHOL

Corn syrup and molasses can be measured with a liquid measuring cup; however, it's often hard to get all of the thick syrup out of the container. If you lightly spray the liquid measuring cup with a vegetable-oil spray, you can get almost all of the corn syrup or molasses out of the cup. These syrups are best measured by weight.

VEGETABLE-OIL SPRAY METHOD

1 cup or 240 ml (8 fl oz) = 12 oz or 336 g

CORN SYRUP OR MOLASSES

2 cups or 1 pint or 480 ml (16 fl oz) =

24 oz or 672 g CORN SYRUP OR MOLASSES

EXTRACTS OR LIQUEURS

Use measuring spoons for extracts, such as almond, vanilla, orange, or lemon, and for small amounts of liqueurs used in these recipes.

1 tsp = 5 ml   1 Tbsp = 15 ml

GEL AND PASTE FOOD COLORS

Gel food colors blend better than paste colors. Paste food colors came out first in the industry. Both are professional-strength food colors. You'll find them more intense than the food coloring available in most grocery stores. Use just a little food color on a toothpick. You'll need even less color when coloring a soft or creamy icing.

Special Decorating Supplies

You'll find most decorating supplies in your local kitchen, cake-decorating, or craft stores or cooking schools. A few hard-to-find products, such as Pettinice RTR Icing, Tylose (C), liquid whitener, gum-paste flowers, silicone molds, petal dust, and lace, rose-leaf, and tulip presses, are available only through specialty houses and distributors. We've listed these sources in the United States, Canada, England, Australia, New Zealand, South Africa, and Zimbabwe. Also check the Internet. You can access 1-800 toll-free calls within the United States and Canada. For suppliers in countries outside the United States and Canada, the country code is in parentheses followed by the city code and then the local phone number.

American Bakels, Inc.
8114 South Hamilton Drive
Little Rock, Arkansas 72209 U.S.A.
Phone: 1 (800) 799-2253
Fax: 1 (501) 568-3947
Pettinice RTR Icing distributor.

Angela's Sugarcraft Equipment
4 White Oak, McLoughlan Avenue
Kensington, Avondale, Harare
ZIMBABWE
Phone: (263) 4 70-3704

Aukland Cake Decorating Supplies
47 Waitakere Road
Waitakere, Auckland NEW ZEALAND
Phone: (64) 9 810-9095
Cake-decorating and sugarcraft.

Beryl's Cake Decorating & Pastry Supplies
P.O. Box 1584
N. Springfield, Virginia 22151 U.S.A.
Website: http://www.beryls.com
Phone: 1 (800) 488-2749
Fax: 1 (703) 750-3779
Stencils, cutters, clay guns, textured rolling pins, Pettinice RTR Icing, Regalice Icing, cake-decorating tools.

B. R. Matthews & Son
12 Gipsey Hill, Crystal Palace
London SE 19 INN   ENGLAND
Phone: (44) 181 670-0788
Cake-decorating and sugarcraft.

Cake Decorating Schools of Australia
Shop 7, Port Phillip Arcade
232 Flinders Street
Melbourne, AUSTRALIA
Phone: (61) 39 654-5335
Cake-decorating and sugarcraft.

Creative Cutters
561 Edwards Avenue, Units 1 & 2
Richmond Hill, Ontario L4C 9W6
CANADA
E-mail: creativecutters@cakeartistry.com
Phone: 1 (905) 883-5638   Voice Mail or Fax: 1 (905) 770-3091
Gum-paste cutters, tools, presses.

Dee Sees Creations, Ltd.
P.O. Box 21
111 Flagstaff
Hamilton   NEW ZEALAND
Phone: (64) 7 854-3039
Cake-decorating and sugarcraft.

Jem Cutters
P.O. Box 115
Kloof 3640   SOUTH AFRICA
1 Gray Place
Pinetown 3610   SOUTH AFRICA
Phone: (27) 31 701-1431
Fax: (27) 31 701-0559
New Jersey (U.S.A.) distributor:
1 (732) 905-0105
Fax: 1 (732) 886-9414
Web: http://www.Jemcutters@aol.com
Tylose C, cutters, and tools.

Kitchen Collectibles
8901 J Street, Suite 2
Omaha, Nebraska 68127 U.S.A.
Phone: 1 (888) 593-2436
Website: http://www.kitchengifts.com
Solid-copper cookie cutters.

New York Cake & Baking
56 West 22nd Street
New York, New York 10010 U.S.A.
Phone: 1 (212) 675-CAKE; that's
1 (212) 675-2253
Cutters, gum-paste tools, textured rolling pins, clay guns, Pettinice RTR Icing, presses.

Orchard Products
51 Hallyburton Road
Hove, East Sussex BN3 7GP
ENGLAND
Phone: (44) 127 341-9418
Sugarcraft cutters and tools.

Petra International
1982 Royal Credit Blvd.
Mississauga, Ontario LSM 4Y1
CANADA
Phone: 1 (800) 261-7226
Website: http://www.pathcom.com/ Petra
Gum-paste flowers.

Sugar Bouquets by Rosemary Watson
23 North Star Drive
Morristown, New Jersey 07960 U.S.A.
Phone: 1 (800) 203-0629
Fax: 1 (973) 538-4939
Lace presses and tulip presses, cutters, and other tools.

Sunflower Sugar Art, Inc.
2637 NW 79th Avenue
Miami, Florida 33122   U.S.A.
Phone: 1 (305) 717-0004
Fax: 1 (305) 717-9905
Lace, rose-leaf, and gum-paste presses, petal dust, and other tools.

Sweet Inspiration Gum Paste Flowers
U.S.A.
Phone: 1 (800) 207-2750
Sprays of gum-paste flowers.

Wilton Enterprises
2240 West 75th Street
Woodridge, Illinois 60517   U.S.A.
Phone: 1 (800) 942-8881
Website: http://www.wilton.com
Baking and cake-decorating supplies.

Index

About the Author

Author Toba M. Garrett is a master cake designer and sugarcraft artist. She has studied the fine art of cake decorating with world-renowned chefs from England, France, Canada, Australia, New Zealand, South Africa, Mexico, and the United States. She attended Le Cordon Bleu in Paris. At Peter Kump's New York School of Culinary Arts, she developed the cake-decorating and confectionery-art curricula and classes that are sold out months in advance.

In her remarkable career, Ms. Garrett has often been recognized for culinary excellence and participated in many international exhibitions. Her culinary artistry has appeared at Bloomingdale's Weddings & Celebrity Weddings showcase and in *Bride's, Gourmet, Essence,* and *Showcase* magazines. She has been featured on television's "Wake Up America" and Lifetime's "Our Home" with Bonnie Montgomery. Her culinary talents were celebrated on WOR-AM radio's "Food Talk," with Arthur Schwartz.

In 1996 she was one of eighteen master chefs chosen to create a showpiece for the 150th birthday celebration of the Smithsonian Museum in Washington, D.C. She has judged many culinary art shows, including the biennial Domaine Carneros Sparkling Wine Wedding Cake Competition.

Ms. Garrett has received many international awards, eight gold medals, six silver medals, three bronze medals, and dozens of diplomas and felicitations with distinction from culinary societies, such as Amicale Culinaire de Washington, D.C.; Les Amis d'Escoffier; Les Dames d'Escoffier; La Saint Michel; and Le Société Culinaire Philanthropique de New York. In 1994 she won the Air France "trip to Paris" prize for wedding-cake designs. In 1996 she won the trophy of Les Commanderie des Cordons Bleus de France for outstanding wedding-cake design. At the 1997 Salon of Culinary Art, she won the competition's highest award, a gold medal from Société des Chefs, Cuisiniers et Pattissiers de la Province de Quebec for outstanding wedding-cake design, and at the 1998 Salon of Culinary Art in New York, she won the 14-karat-gold medal-of-honor grand prize for pastry.

She is a member of ICES, former president of the Confectionery Arts Guild of New Jersey, and former member of the British Sugarcraft Guild.

Ms. Garrett was educated at Fordham University and City College of New York in communications, theater, and fine arts. Before becoming a full-time culinary artist, she taught computer science and business education for the New York City Board of Education and Higher Education. She has studied floral design at Parsons School of Design. She holds a master's in educational and instructional technology from Long Island University.

Toba Garrett's wedding cake and cookie designs. This photo by Rita Maas first appeared in *Essence* magazine in June 1997.